# THE ULTIMATE GUIDE FOR PHARMACEUTICAL REPS

ANDY FARAH, M.D.

The Ultimate Guide for Pharmaceutical Reps
An Advanced Manual for Reps Who Excel



ISBN: 0-9678437-1-5

Library of Congress
Catalog Card Number: 00-90424

Printed in the United States by:
Morris Publishing
3212 East Highway 30
Kearney, NE 68847
1-800-650-7888

# *Table of Contents*

## Part III
## Strategies for the Tough Sells



## Part IV
## The Next Level

*"Detailing physicians is an art form to be refined and improved with every call, over an entire career..."*

Dr. John Goeke,
psychologist and sales consultant

# *Introduction: Selling Health*

You may not have considered your job in this way before, but you are privileged as a salesperson. You sell what few can, you sell health.

Over 200 people may have applied for your job and you were the one selected, because you have the skills necessary to engage physician customers and provide the latest medical information that will be used to help hundreds and possibly thousands of people in your territory.

But selling health is no easy task. For example, I prescribe over a thousand antidepressants each year, and despite my extensive warnings about discontinuing them, the number one reason for a depression relapse is "I was doing so well I thought I could just stop the medicine..."

Like me, you don't want your message to fall on deaf ears. That's why I wrote this book. It is designed to help you get your message out, help you make an impact, and help you succeed as a rep. And that means your whole company will be successful selling health. You are the foot soldier who gets the information out, and in most cases, you are the only link the doctors and health care providers have with a pharmaceutical company. I once asked a sales training director what qualities he looked for in potential reps, and his answer was "someone who can handle the responsibility of being our company's liaison to any and every health care worker they meet."

That's quite a responsibility, but again, you were hired because you have the skills necessary to handle it, and the skills needed to handle the routine stresses of a sales job, *plus* the challenges posed by selling to your unique customer base.

So, good luck with your sales of health. I hope this book enhances your career for years to come.

# *About This Book*

As you know, this book is written from the perspective of your customer. I am the doctor that you call on every day. For seven years my focus of research has been medical decision making, and in particular, the process by which we physicians choose one prescription drug over another. Much of that research is included in this book. Many strategies are discussed, so choose the best ones for your style and your product.

When I was a resident, because of a scheduling fluke, I had the misfortune of presenting the same case three days in a row to three different attending doctors. The case involved a lady who had frequent chest pains or "angina" that felt exactly like a heart attack; but during every hospital admission, her heart always checked out fine. Being the psychiatry resident on call, I was asked to interview her and determine if her illness was psychosomatic.

I then told her history to each of the three doctors on three consecutive days. The first was an anxiety disorder specialist. He concluded that the patient had "atypical panic attacks" which caused her chest pains, and he recommended an antianxiety agent. The second attending doctor was a neuropsychiatrist, who learned that she had a stroke some years ago, and he believed that due to the precise location of the stroke she would obviously have some anxiety symptoms that would account for her episodic chest pain. The third doctor specialized in family and marriage therapy. He was interested to hear that the patient's son was in prison on drug charges and believed this stress was the cause of her psychosomatic illness, as her son's criminal behavior had "broken her heart."

Who was correct? Possibly all three. But as a resident, I learned to listen to many different perspectives, and choose the ones that made the most sense for each situation and worked the best for the patient.

This case also demonstrates that sometimes in medicine, there is not always one right answer. You've found this to be true of you job as well. And you will continue to encounter many situations over your career that will require some creativity or new strategy you hadn't planned on. This book is designed to prepare you for the routine and not so routine situations to come.

So don't be afraid to try something new that is outside the "'text book approach." Take what you think will help your sales and apply it! Follow these guidelines and you'll avoid the chest pains.

1. Feel free to skip around. This book can be read start to finish or chapters can be read out of order. So if you want to look up a specific topic, go ahead. I'll direct you to other parts that may be helpful throughout. I know a few things about your schedules, and I know "sitting down and reading a book cover to cover just for fun" isn't usually blocked off on your calendars.

2. Bounce ideas off your colleagues! You can do this on a one to one basis or at district meetings. Some districts assign each rep a chapter or two for a summarized report at meetings. And you thought book report days were over...

3. Take notes in the margins. Specifically, write down the names of your doctors that come to mind when you explore each section. This will help recall and help you think in practical day to day terms about these strategies.

When I have surveyed physicians to ask what kind of detail they want from reps, most of them say they are looking for information they can use day to day that will make a difference for their patients. That's what we want from you, and likewise, I plan to provide you with same type of practical information and selling strategies that you can use every day.

Part I will tell you the basics, such as the essential elements of the detail and how to overcome the common obstacles you will face in the course of your day. After discussing the main influences on prescription habits, some strategies of top performing reps are shared.

Part II will provide you with advanced information on how your customer is thinking. You'll also learn the way doctors would like you to close your sale, and the secret to getting invited back to any office.

Part III will help you with some of the tougher sales situations, while Part IV is designed to help take your career to "the next level," extending your influence beyond the traditional one to one detail.

Finally, the book will give you information about seminars and unique rep training opportunities. So read on, and remember to grab a pen...

# A Word About *The Doctor As Customer*

The book that precedes this text, *The Doctor as Customer*, is a basic introduction to the physician customer. It may have been required reading as part of your initial training. The book you are holding, however, is more detailed.

If you missed *The Doctor as Customer*, don't sweat it. You'll still get a lot out of this book. And the information in Chapter 3 ("The Top Obstacles You Face") is covered in both books, because this was voted the "most helpful chapter" by readers of the first edition of *The Doctor as Customer.*

# *Part I*

# *The Basics of Selling to Doctors*

*chapter*

# 1 Getting the Doctor's Attention and Changing Prescription Habits

Your job preparation is excellent. I have met with many of your sales training directors and their staffs, and I would tell you how impressed I am, even if I wasn't trying to sell them books. You are trained to sell by the best.

And, your product knowledge is outstanding. I've helped write some of the tests you took on your drug's "mechanism of action," so I know how tough they are. All of this study is designed to make you an expert on a select group of medications. Then you are prepared to educate physician customers and help countless people benefit from the latest medical knowledge.

Yet, once you've completed your extensive preparation, the most challenging aspects of your job are still ahead of you: first — you must get the attention of a customer who is time pressured (and may even have a bit of an ego), and secondly, act as a catalyst for change in that customer's daily habits — that is, prescription habits. Sometimes you must accomplish all this in less than two minutes!

Your two main challenges are:

1. Getting your customer's attention.
2. Effecting a change in your customer's habits.

## *I. Getting Our Attention:*

I recently treated a very complicated patient in our hospital. She had a severe and life threatening reaction to one of her medications, but the problem was, nobody was sure which one. It could have been the anti-convulsant she was taking, the antipsychotic, or her blood pressure medication. To further complicate things, she listed haloperidol (and all others in its class) and lithium as "allergies." Now, to *really* complicate things, she was manic. I mean with a capital M. She couldn't sleep, talked excessively, was paranoid, and would sing hymns all day — and very loudly. She even lost her voice, but she kept belting out *"will the circle be unbroken..."* in a gravel filled Rod Stewart kind of voice. Oh yes, one more thing, she was prone to violence. She struck another patient, and even attacked a visiting sales rep on the ward (just kidding about that second assault...).

Now, I'm a pretty sharp psychiatrist, but this poor lady was one of the sickest patients I've seen, and though a list of medications could have helped her, 90% of them were contraindicated because of her prior med reaction. The hospital administrators wanted her fixed yesterday, the family wanted her fixed and sent to a supervised living situation (in another state), and the nurses were insisting I transfer her to another hospital (none of the other local facilities were thrilled with the idea).

Every day on rounds, for three weeks, it seemed that everyone was telling me what to do. "Try this drug!" or "Send her to hospital X!" and the dreaded hospital administrator's question: "Can't you fix her faster than usual?" ("Gee, I never thought of that, thanks for the tip!") But each day I evaluated the risks involved in giving various medications and weighed them against the risks of not giving them (including risks to staff, other patients). Now, I'm always happy to get ideas, but in this case, none of the advice givers really appreciated the fact that she had been in the intensive care unit for three weeks because of a medication reaction. Since I had consulted on the case when she was in the ICU, I knew a great deal about the situation. I had also phoned her mother several times to get the facts straight regarding which medications caused true allergic reactions and what her baseline behavior was like. So all the daily advice was essentially just distracting background noise. During morning rounds for three weeks we were treated to raspy hymns. Her case was obviously not progressing very quickly...

But when my partner Joel said, "You might try quetiapine, it's structurally unrelated to the drugs she's allergic to," I listened to him. And I took his advice.

Why? How did he manage to get my attention and influence my prescription when no one else could? Because:

- **A Relationship Was Established:**

  That's why your first priority should be building a relationship with your physician customers. When you walk in you want to be greeted as a friend, not "just another rep." And eventually, you'll become a partner in the business of patient care. We don't always have time for reps, but we always make time for friends. Because Joel is a friend, he has instant access to me. Of all the people that day who gave me advice, I listened only to one.

- **Credibility Through Understanding the Process:**

  Joel's had his share of tough cases, and had a pretty good idea of what my thought process was. Keep in mind that there is a clinical analysis behind every prescription decision. Knowing the process behind our decisions will give you more credibility. (So consider a preceptorship whenever it is offered.)

  Also, Joel has demonstrated a superior medical knowledge in the past, and has treated similar cases with good results. You too have a superior knowledge, so don't be shy when expressing your understanding of diseases and products. When you teach us, you help our patients.

- **Practical Information Was Given:**

  My partner gave me advice that was usable and practical. Sure, he charged me a consulting fee, and maybe he's not such a pal after all, but his advice worked!

- **The Right Time and Place:**
  My partner and I discussed this case back at the office with no distractions, not on the ward among the hymns. Pick your detail times and settings carefully — avoid meetings in the hall between patients and seek opportunities and places where distractions are minimal.

Now, lets visit the case above one more time. Let's say I tried Joel's advice, and the patient didn't improve, in fact, she got worse, and began singing all night as well (and even off key!). I would conclude that it simply wasn't the right medication for this patient, but he had no way of knowing this, and I may even ask him what he thinks I should do next. Let's say that the same advice came from a patient's managed care company. (It is actually common for these companies to phone and give treatment directives, and many will even refuse to pay for hospitalizations if their orders are ignored.) If the patient gets worse on their advice, I'd see it as further proof that managed care is harmful to patients and destructive to the medical profession. Obviously, my relationship with the advice giver will contribute to my attitude about the results. Again, developing a good relationship with your doctors always comes first.

## *II. Becoming A Catalyst for Change:*

The second part of your job is even more daunting than the first. You are asked to change someone's prescribing habits. Changing a habit is never easy. Even if a person is motivated to change a habit, it is still a tough job. It demands motivation and constant attention. The physicians you call on in the course of your day will most likely not be motivated to change, unless you convince them it is worth the effort.

At a recent seminar I was speaking about this problem when a drug rep asked, "Dr. Farah, as a psychiatrist, how do you change habits in your patients?" Good question!

"Well," I replied, "I make them think it's *their* idea." I explained that each patient must realize that it is in their best interest to change the habit. My role is to frame the options so that they recognize they'd be better off. Simply asking (or telling) someone to change a habit rarely works.

For example, I've asked my father to change a habit for 20 years. He has watched CBS news as long as I can remember. The only problem is, he despises CBS news. He has cursed Dan Rather and called him a communist since before I knew what a communist was. But for some reason he turns on Dan every night. It's just his habit. It seems quite unpleasant to me, and I've told him about NBC and ABC news, but night after night he curses the Kremlin Broadcast Network and Premier Vladymir Rather.

Your customers may also have some habits that they themselves don't even like. But old habits do die hard. I've tried everything with Dad, but when I visit him next month I know at 6:30 every night we have a date with Comrade Rather. I'm not a very effective catalyst for change in this scenario, but luckily my advice works better on your customers than my family.

Here are the ways you can become an effective catalyst of change in the prescription habits of your customers:

- **Use Informed Reasoning:**

  It's no secret that in order to influence others, you must use knowledge and reason. And the most effective strategy for influencing change involves letting the customer draw the conclusions. You provide the data, both of you reason through it, and the customer decides what it all means. Let me show you how this works: I recently had lunch with a rep who has this technique mastered. She asked me to describe the weight gain I observed with the newer antipsychotics. Then she discussed the data based on these drug trials and we compared it to my clinical experience. I realized that the literature supports my observation that weight gain was negligible with drug X, which she sells, but she didn't have to tell me that.

- **Focus on What is Best for the Patient:**

  If you want credibility, and you want real success, then take these words to heart — your message and your relationship with the customer are tools by which you help the patient. If your message helps the patient, your sales will follow.

- **Point Out What Makes Your Drug Easy for the Doc to Use:**
  You can discuss advantages of a product all day, but that won't change habits unless you give it personal meaning. Remember to make the issues relevant. Ease of dosing *means* patients are more compliant, a low incidence of side effects *means* fewer phone calls to the doc. Make your detail stand out by coupling advantages of the product with advantages to the prescriber of that product.

Now, I can visit Dad anytime to see if my informed reasoning (...if all the networks are controlled by Commies, why not change channels and keep an eye on all of them?), advocacy stance (...your blood pressure and requirement for bourbon will be reduced if you avoid Dan Blather), and other advice worked. But how do you know if you've helped effect a change in your customer's habit?

After you finish a great detail, you have to wait for the prescription data to tell the story. What if you find yourself waiting a month or two and nothing changes? The doc has heard the message, maybe more than once, but still does not change his or her prescription pattern. I know none of you have experienced this (!) but I'll review the dilemma just in case it arises.

The top reasons your docs may not change their prescription habits after a detail:

1. Despite adequate information, **the doc lacks the experience they need to feel comfortable using the product.** What can you do about this? On your next detail, find out what their experience has been thus far, even if limited. Let them know if their dosing is correct and if results are in line with what is expected. If they have none, then borrow the experiences of others and tell them about how others in the community are using and receiving the product. In Chapter 9 I'll discuss other ways you can be certain your product moves into the mental "comfort zone" of frequent use.

2. **A bad experience with the product** has occurred that they have not shared with you. Ask them about any problems they may have seen using the drug. More on this situation in Chapter 6.

3. **They still doubt the efficacy of the product.** So, show them the data! Tell them some success stories and do what you can to remind them that double-blind placebo-controlled studies *are* the gold standard for efficacy in medicine.

4. **Ambivalence about the dosing or some basic aspect of using the drug.** This happens a lot when there is a dose range rather than a target

dose for a drug. But never hesitate to run down the basics of the drug's use. If you're concerned about insulting the doc's intelligence, then phrase it like this: "I know you're aware of this already, but drug X is dosed once a day, at 20 mg, and it's usually given in the morning..."

5. Finally, as Dad says, never rule out the possibility of communist infiltration of your territory.

It is also equally important to detail when things are going well for your product. Too often, we tend to focus on what to do when sales are down, not what to do when they are up.

Here are some tips:

- Drop by just to say thanks for the support.
- Tell your best customers first about new data or information.
- Ask them if you can quote their positive comments about your product.
- Visit them at least as often as any other doc, probably more. The main point is not to slack off because things are going well. Remember, sales are good *because* of your efforts.

*chapter*

# 2 The Essential Aspects of the Detail and the HITEC Model:

*Essential: indispensable; that which is necessary.*

What are the essential elements that make up a complete product detail? To answer this question, I went straight to your customers:

My survey of 300 primary care providers asked:

**"What is the most important thing a rep can tell you about their product?"**

## *The #1 Response:*

**Tell me how to use this drug.**

Sounds pretty simple doesn't it? But the fact is, we prescribe drugs that we are comfortable using. If one important piece of prescribing information is missing, (such as once or twice a day dosing, maximum approved dose, or what time of day to take the drug), we may avoid using it altogether. There is no room for uncertainty when prescribing medicines, so we stick with what we are certain of. Sometimes the avoidance is even subconscious, that is, a doctor may simply not use a product, and never stop to consider why. They just prescribe others in the class, and never think of that choice consciously when prescribing.

Now I know it seems silly to say "only give the drug once a day" if you think it's a fundamental piece of data that everyone should know by now, but the reality is, if I don't know something so fundamental, I may not ask it! We may be simply embarrassed to ask a simple question, so don't be afraid to just say the basics.

## *The #2 Response:*

**What are the side effects?**

This is another way of saying "How much trouble is this drug going to be when I prescribe it? How many phone calls will I get?" The best way to discuss side effects is to always elaborate on what to do about them. Even placebo pills have side effects, even though imaginary. As reps, you shouldn't feel the need to downplay side effects. You may lose credibility if you prepare your customer for a particular percentage and they observe a higher rate of the side effect. Shift your focus to how to deal with side effects. Tell us what to do about them and we'll no longer be intimidated by them.

Your job is to arm us with knowledge, to move us into a comfort zone of use, which you'll learn all about in Chapter 9. Being comfortable with a product means knowing when to say "try taking it with food, that will reduce the chance of stomach upset," or "take half a tablet in the morning and half at bedtime to reduce sedation."

Doctors want a drug that's easy to use. That means knowing what trouble to look for and how to handle it.

## *The #3 Response:*

**What are the illnesses that can benefit from the drug?**

Simple? Right? Well, not always. These are the days of anticonvulsant prescriptions to reduce chronic pain, and antidepressants to treat PMS. We practice in confusing "off label" times, and exactly what the new drugs work for can be complicated, especially when primary care physicians consider using specialty drugs. In my community, there were three speaker programs this month. All were sponsored by makers of antidepressants, but none were about depression. One dealt with Panic Disorder, one with Obsessive-Compulsive Disorder, and another focused on Attention Deficit Disorder. Confusing times...

The survey responders who believed it was most important to hear about drug indications didn't need clarification of the drug's FDA approval — this information is well publicized. They were curious about indications they may not be aware of, new research, or maybe some patient profiles that could benefit from the drug. They said, in effect, tell us something *new* that will help our patients.

## *The #4 Response:*

**What is the cost?**

Confusing times indeed — some drug cards have co-pays that are often higher than the cost of the generic medication itself, and don't mention "preferred formularies." But isn't this a patient concern? Why are so many doctors interested in cost?

Two main reasons: if a patient can't afford a drug, they will not stay on it. This can obviously have dramatic consequences. I admitted a lady to the hospital this week who became depressed and suicidal. The chart showed that she had been stable for a year, but about a month before she tried to cut costs by cutting her antidepressant dose in half (relapse rates double when the dose is lowered). The only drug I've ever seen anyone sacrifice all their money for, and even go thousands of dollars in debt for is cocaine (and OK, maybe Viagra).

The other reason docs are so interested in cost is really another version of "how much trouble is the drug for *me*, the one who is prescribing it?" When the pharmacists says "this drug is not on your plan, and that will be $90" and the patient goes to a pay phone outside the pharmacy, they are not calling their insurance carrier, and they are not calling their benefits manager at the plant to gripe about the lousy prescription plan he bought, they are calling me! They make it our problem.

That's why your detail should include some mention of a drug's cost. Docs just want to have this information. But never use the word "cheap" in the discussion. Talk about a drug as a "good value," or priced competitively. Cheap sounds, well, cheap...

## *The #5 Response:*

**What is the Experience!**

Doctors want to know what the clinical experience has been before they prescribe a product. Eventually, their own clinical experience will grow and it will then become the main factor in determining whether they use more of the product. But in order to be comfortable initially prescribing a drug, we need to know what others have seen.

Many products have been available in other countries before their launches. This experience can provide you with a wealth of data to talk about. Market shares, because they reflect the activity of thousands of prescribers, are usually of great interest to your docs.

**Summary of the H-I-T-E-C Model:**

**H** — **How** do I use this drug?
**I** — What are the **Indications**?
**T** — How much **Trouble** is it for me to use?
**E** — What's the **Experience** been like with the drug?
**C** — Tell me the **Cost**!!!

If you hit all these elements, you've covered what the majority of docs say they want to hear. You'll find that the

HITEC model is a good framework to operate from in any setting. In fact, I use it in my speaker programs. When I lecture on antidepressants, antipsychotics, or medications for Alzheimer's, I always have this outline in front of me, and with this guide, I know my remarks are complete.

"I'm sure you're wondering, Dr. Perry, what advantages do *BatPills* have for my patients?"

*chapter*

# 3 The Top Obstacles You Face

Your sales mission is full of obstacles and you must prepare to overcome them if your goal is to excel.

There are two major types of obstacles that prevent you from getting your message across and effecting a change in prescription habits: there are obstacles that exist as a routine part of the medical practice day, and there are obstacles that exist in the minds of your docs.

As you were reading that last sentence, you probably thought of several docs in your territory that have demonstrated a mindset that was resistant to change or even resistant to hearing new information.

I recently lectured at a district meeting where a rep asked "What should I say to a doc who told me that he wouldn't use my product until he saw data about changes in the rat brain serotonin receptors after five years of exposure to the drug?"

I said "Tell him he's an idiot." Even if such a study is underway, why would anyone wait five years before they use the product? The guy was simply being difficult. Unfortunately, the rep was in no position to tell the customer what I thought of him (but it would have felt great!). We'll discuss this under "Obstacle 4," and there's more detail on difficult customers in Chapter 15. Hopefully, the customers you thought of who have obstinate minds aren't this ridiculous...

## *Obstacle 1: Access!*

To *influence* your customer, you have to first *get* to your customer! I don't need to tell you what a challenge this can be. You will also find that every office is different, and even within the same office group, each doctor will approach rep visits differently. In my practice, Dr. M. refuses to see reps at all, Dr. W. will allow visits while he is eating lunch, Dr. V. will let them schedule visits in his appointment book (but if a patient wants the spot, he'll give it to them and may not tell the rep they've been canceled until they show up!); while *I* invite them into my office anytime and make them buy books for their whole district before I listen to the detail. And then there's Dr. B., who is, well, rep-*hostile*! No kidding. Imagine the "Soup Nazi" with a script pad (same accent too). "You've been telling me the same garbage for four years! Out of my sight you infidel!" is how one rep described the encounter with the Script-Nazi in his debriefing. (There will be more Script-Nazi stories later.) We run the gamut in our one office.

You'll often find that a key office person will control access to the doctors. Knowing that person and treating him or her well can make access a given. People who hire me for speaker programs, articles, or seminars, quickly learn that Nadine is the key person who controls my schedule. In our clinical office, Marisa is the key to seeing the doctors. The reps in our community have learned their real mission is to keep these two young ladies happy.

When I was interviewing for a residency spot at a famous and prestigious institution, I asked if I could meet the famous Dr. so-and-so, and explained that I had read all of his articles and books. "No," the department chairman told me, "He was here, you see, but his wife was unhappy once they moved to this town, and well, when his wife was unhappy, *everybody* was unhappy..." Yes, even one of the most accomplished physicians in the world has to keep the key person happy.

## *Solution:*

The easiest fix is simply to ask the doctor when exactly is the best time to detail. Accept the answer and use it, even if it is outside the office. But, the BEST fix is to build a great working relationship with each of your docs. Take the time to really learn about your customers, their personal likes, their families, and of course, learn all you can about their practices. This will lay the groundwork for relationship based selling.

As I mentioned in Chapter 1, we always make time for friends. Develop a relationship that will require no appointments.

## *Obstacle 2: Time Pressure*

Let me describe what one routine day was like for me. I am a psychiatrist so this will describe a typical psychiatric practice; however, all doctors have to deal with the problem of time pressure.

To start the morning, I made hospital rounds. This involved seeing and evaluating the status of 14 inpatients between the hours of 7:30 and 11:00 a.m. (The average number of patients I have in the hospital at any time is usually six, but this was a busy week.) The caseload involved the usual mix of schizophrenics who were psychotic (when suffering from an exacerbation in this illness, a patient will have hallucinations or delusions), dementia patients (such as those with Alzheimer's, who are usually hospitalized when they are so confused as to be dangerous), and substance abusers who need detox. There are also depressed individuals who need hospitalization to prevent them from committing suicide. Sounds like an uplifting start to any day, doesn't it!

Well, there were uplifting parts, as four of the patients were improved enough to go home. There were even humorous parts: one particular woman had been committed against her will (i.e., court ordered to be hospitalized due to the dangerousness of her behavior), and her commitment papers actually read "The respondent has manic depressive illness and has been off her lithium. She went to buy a car, and when they told her she could not afford it she got mad and started jumping up and down on the roof of the car until the police came. She screamed at them and said she wanted the car for free..." Upon meeting her, I told her there would be no charge for the hospital stay.

Another man demanded to be discharged as soon as I met him. He had been hospitalized many times and knew all the right jargon, and then some. I asked him if had suicidal thoughts, and he screamed "I don't have any thoughts of suicide, I don't have any thoughts of homicide and I don't even have any thoughts of *genocide*!"

During the course of these hospital rounds, my beeper went off twelve times, people kept sticking papers under my nose to sign, and I even got a visit from one of those hospital PR people. She wanted to know if I'd do an interview for local TV about how a person may get "traumatized by dog bites..." I said something like "you must be kidding" and she got the hint. By lunch time, I was already behind and feeling pressured by the never-ending crunch of paperwork. Lunch involved several animal crackers and a coke. Then I began the office phase of my practice.

During the next five hours, I saw fifteen outpatients, filled out seven insurance forms, returned twelve phone calls from patients, patients' families, administrators, and insurance companies trying to deny care to some of my patients. At 5:30, I returned to the hospital to see consultations that were called in during the day (these patients were on the medical ward of the hospital, not the psychiatric one, but still needed a psychiatric evaluation). One of these was a young girl who overdosed after breaking up with her boyfriend, and another was an elderly lady with dementia whose judgment was impaired, so I was asked to help determine her level of competency.

I finally left about 7:30. On the way home I was paged by two pharmacies to tell me that some of the prescriptions I had written during the day were "not on that patient's insurance company's preferred list" and they asked me if I "wouldn't mind changing them to something else."

And this is a typical day for me.

The obvious obstacle: how can you fit into this kind of busy schedule and have a meaningful impact?

## *Solution:*

This problem of too little time is nothing new. It's probably not going to change much in the foreseeable future as managed care constraints increase the workload for all of us. But, while I may not be able to find the time to see a drug rep, I can almost always *make* time to see my friends. Again, the answer comes down to building a personal relationship. Not only will this get you in the door, but it will get you quality time.

I know that relationship building is not always an easy task. There are certainly many physicians who are aloof or even not very pleasant to be around. Despite all the different personalities out there, you have to find a way to engage them. If nothing else, approach each call with the understanding of the doctor's typical day. Sometimes, the best thing you can say is, "Doc, I know you're busy today but I just wanted to see if there's anything you need?" Sounds trite, but we'd rather hear *those* words than a sales pitch that we probably won't remember because we're too worried about getting to the next patient.

And again, remember your best selling may occur outside the office, at the dinner program, the professional meeting, or a private meal with just you and the doc. If there is no quality time available, it's up to you to create some.

## *Obstacle 3: Information Overload!*

As you know from your own medical and product studies, there seems to be an infinite amount of scientific information out there. I find myself searching Medline for information about twice a week. I searched "depression" today to get a data base to work from, and over 22,000 articles popped up! Though some articles are obscure, and some are important, there sure are plenty. I work hard to keep up to date, and try to publish about two or three articles a year. But despite my efforts, there are several current journals on my desk that will be out of date before I get a chance to open them.

Now, you may think your career is in sales, but you are really an educator. And your challenge is to make your message stand out among all the other medical data out there.

## *Solution:*

Think of your job as not simply presenting the educational information, but making it relevant to us, specifically to our practices. For example, I asked a rep last week about the possibility that her product, a sleep aid, might cause withdrawal effects when stopped. She came in later that day with a study showing no such problems after a year of daily use. I was so pleased, that I made several copies of the paper to give to my partners.[1] This paper answered *my* specific concern.

But what if you're not sure *what* their specific needs are? I've interviewed numerous doctors on the topic of exactly what we want from reps, and most say "give me practical and useful information..." and, the information that will help our patients is at your fingertips. So focus on the most practical aspects of the educational materials. Since I may not have time to find the pearls in the article, highlight the useful parts as you present.

## *Obstacle 4: "...But doctor, you're wrong!"*

I recently gave a CME lecture on treatment resistant depression. I had told the audience that a blood pressure medication, pindolol, could be used to augment certain antidepressant therapies. I explained how it worked and

---

[1] (I even gave a copy of the article to the Script-Nazi, who called me a "puppet handing out propaganda.")

how to use the drug in combination with others. During the question and answer time a doc commented that I was wrong about pindolol, and said that he had read studies that said "it was not an augmentation strategy but an agent that acts as an antidepressant all by itself." Only one problem, he was dead wrong. Now, at the time I am writing this, pindolol has been used to augment several antidepressants, and there hasn't been a study to test his theory that it acts alone as an antidepressant. Now, this guy may be way ahead of his time or maybe he's been lucky once or twice trying this... but I doubt it. So, what did I say?

1. Thanks for your comment, anyone else have a question or comment?
2. I'm unaware of those studies, please tell us if this is something you have observed...
3. You're an idiot. If you check the literature, you will see that this strategy has never been reported...

Yes, response #2 was correct, though response #3 is very tempting. Particularly since he started his comment by telling me *I* was wrong. But remember this first rule when dealing with someone who is wrong and may even be contentious: don't let your emotions get the better of you. If you sound angry or irritated, it will detract from your message and you will probably seem defensive to others. Besides, why challenge or embarrass this guy in front of his home crowd? When someone's beliefs are way off, you need to figure out where they come from. Once this guy spoke some more, it was clear he just misunderstood the studies. Fortunately, I had a review article with me and shared it with the crowd. I also took his card and sent him copies of my file on augmentation strategies. He needed to further study this topic in private, not public.

Fortunately, most of the physicians I know *do* handle their ego strength appropriately, but it can still make your job tougher. When you hear a physician simply misstate some information about your product, you'll be tempted to respond like I described in #3 above, but there are better ways:

## *Solution:*

First, get Dr. Ego to talk about the product. If they have a false belief, as in the above example, try to find out where it came from. Also, minds are often best changed by one's own arguments. For example, a false belief about a product's efficacy can mean no prescriptions at all. If a doctor says "Drug X just does not work..." tell them you really would like to hear their specific experience. Once they start talking they will probably reveal that they concluded the drug was non-effective after only a few patient trials, maybe just one! They may also reveal that they tried the product on treatment resistant patients (who had responded to no other drugs). But the key is, DON'T TELL THEM THIS, make them say it and allow them to realize it.

Secondly, get them talking very specifically about how they use the product. They may be dosing it wrong. I recall one doctor telling me he had no luck with an antianxiety agent. He had picked one with an eight hour half life, and told his patients to take it at bedtime... in the morning when they woke, they were nervous... no kidding.

## *Obstacle 5: The Bad Experience*

All the best research and marketing in the world can be undone by one patient's bad experience.

I was at a seminar recently in which this question came up: the rep explained that he and a particular doctor were good friends and even went golfing together often. Yet, the doctor had one patient experience anaphylactic shock while on this rep's drug and he's never tried it again (in over three years!). The relationship is great. Such an allergic reaction can happen in anyone, even to an aspirin, but the doctor forever associates this reaction with his drug. How in the world do you overcome that?

## *Solution:*

First, keep doing what this rep did — continue on with the relationship. Don't write them off because they've not prescribed your drug in a while. This solidifies that either you don't care, or the drug really *is* trouble, or both. Your continued presence and support will eventually pay off. You never know what future event (an expert's opinion, an article, or a colleague's comment) may sway their opinion in favor of your product, and you need to help keep it in their mind as an option.

Second, if they bring up the bad experience, then go ahead and remind them of the odds. They had the privilege of treating that "one in ten thousand patients" we've always read about. What are the odds it will happen again? (My friend Gregg insists that I am the safest person to fly with. Why? Because I've survived a plane crash. What are the odds of two crashes in one lifetime?)

Also, you can also utilize the medical support you have at your corporate office. The fact is, odd reactions scare us because they are a realm of uncertainty, outside the expected comfort zone of usage, so again, the only way to combat this is with knowledge.

Don't make it worse by minimizing the episode or challenging their experience. Comments like "I've never heard of *that* before" are a challenge to the doc reporting it. The best stance is one of interest, seek as much detail as possible and let them talk about the case. It may be harder to pinpoint your drug as the culprit. Never forget the question "was the patient on any other medicine at the time of this reaction?" Sometimes it is a combination of medicines, not a single one that causes a problem.

Remember that the real reason we are avoiding your drug after a bad reaction is fear. A doc will fear a problem that he or she doesn't know what to do about. The reason we do a residency is so we are ready for anything once we're turned out of school. A good residency will prepare you for anything you may see, no matter how rare, and give you the insight to know when to consult a doctor in another specialty. Think of yourself as an extension of that education process. Give us enough knowledge to dispel whatever fears we have about your product.

Finally, when all else fails, don't be ashamed to settle for your drug being "pigeon-holed" into a particular category. If a bad experience means the doc only uses drug X if "three others have failed..." so be it. Better to have a small role than none at all.

## *Obstacle 6: The Script-Nazi!*

Somewhere out there, one of you lucky reps has to detail the Script-Nazi. That insufferable, gruff, possibly psychotic, and certainly rep-hostile doctor. Another favorite story goes like this:

The rep tries his best to detail, all the while the Script-Nazi rubs his eyes, and then after a few minutes of silence mutters "you insist on doing it, every time, don't you?"

"What's that?" the rep asks

"You insist on turning my office into a *den of lies*!!... get out of my sight, you infidel!"

Wow, you have to detail the last remaining psychiatrist from the Third Reich...

## *Solution:*

Learn to goose step. Just kidding. It's not that hopeless. You see, though the Script-Nazi is rep-hostile, he actually considers me a friend (maybe not after the publication of this book, however). For my favorite reps, who have marching orders to detail him, they get special access. (He is actually very busy and out-prescribes all the other doctors in the five surrounding counties, so he's at the top of everyone's list.) I am the middle man, I'll introduce them and chat for a while with them until he softens up. He rarely acts badly in front of another doctor and he does smile occasionally, and once he even said "thank you for lunch." So, the key to the impossible detail is getting a buddy on the inside, you infidels...

**Summary of How to Overcome Common Obstacles:**

1. A good relationship can mean access. A great relationship with a doc will mean instant access. In the meantime, find out who controls access and keep them happy.

2. All of your customers are under time pressure, so look for opportunities to sell outside the office.

3. Make your information stand out among all the other medical data by linking it with each doctor's clinical practice.

4. When the customer is misinformed, provide the facts so they will see the error.

5. Bad experiences with products should be handled with knowledge. The more we know, the less we fear.

6. If your list includes the Script-Nazi (or someone similar), get a buddy on the inside, and good luck...

## *The Last Word:*

The key person in _______________'s office is _________. Can you answer this question for all your doctors?

*chapter*

# 4 The Main Influence on Prescription Habits

After years of research into medical decision making, what have we found to be the main influence when choosing one drug over another?

## The Doctor's Personal Experience With the Product

Here's an example of how personal experience can influence medical decisions:

During one long call night as an intern, I was asked to evaluate a paranoid lady in the emergency room. She went into great detail about how the CIA was going to kill her (they had been tracking her with satellites). She held a tattered newspaper up to the florescent lights to demonstrate the secret messages that were encrypted therein, which instructed agents on how to finish her off. I listened patiently and then told her she was in no danger, and that these fears were the result of paranoia from her mental illness. I told her that I could help, if she agreed to come into the hospital and take some medication. How did my little speech go? Let's just say I'm glad the security officer was standing outside the room. (I had exposed that I was "one of them" and of course the medication was really poison, so she shoved me and made a break for the exit.)

This patient needed an antipsychotic, and fast. So I ran down the list of those that came in intramuscular form, and picked one. Fortunately it worked well and she stabilized in a short time. Because using that drug resulted in almost immediate safety for all involved, I used it repeatedly during future call nights.

Experience really is the greatest teacher. Now that I've progressed far beyond internship, when I talk to a paranoid person I listen patiently, use a variety of strategies to help them, but I don't immediately tell them that they are paranoid. I also find it helps to throw in empathetic comments, such as, "yes, anyone would agree that your district manager is a tyrannical fascist who has dedicated his life to your destruction."

When it comes to the psychology of prescribing one product over another, there is no greater influence than all the memories in my head of how other patients responded — or didn't respond — to a drug. All medical judgments are based on a combination of knowledge and experience. You provide the knowledge, but the experience can only come from my day to day practice.

But it's not that simple — because I saw 18 hospitalized patients today, and one consultation (and I'm writing this on a Saturday!). When I got a page a few minutes ago, I was told Mrs. J. was febrile. She was already taking an antibiotic. It may not be doing the job, or maybe she has caught a terrible hospital borne resistant bug — but whether my impression of the drug now is positive or negative, the point is, I wrote numerous orders for numerous drugs today, and I can't remember which antibiotic I had prescribed last week for her.

This may sound odd, but you may have to help me remember my experiences with your product. Keep in mind your drug is one of many I may use in the course of a week. When was the last time your customer decided to sit back and reflect on a drug? Without the right line of questioning, probably never.

Another key point is, the generalizations we make about drugs are based on a limited number of experiences. I recently had a discussion with one of my partners about lamotrigine. This is a new anticonvulsant that we both have tried on our manic depressive patients. I've tried it twice, and I thought it helped both patients greatly. He tried it once, and believed it actually exacerbated the patient's mania. In one of my hospital team meetings, a nurse asked me what I thought of using this drug for mania, and I said it was "a wonderful new option." My patients responded at fairly low doses, and had minimal side effects. She said "now I'm confused..." — my partner had told her in the previous hour's meeting that the drug would do more harm than good! We made our generalizations, and even influenced (or confused) other clinicians based on a sample size of three patients!

Remember this lesson when a generalization is made about your product. And go ahead and ask, "what was the sample size?"

**Making the Most of Personal Experience:**

- Prescriptions of a product will increase after a patient takes it and does well, and if overall the use results in a good experience for both the doc and patient.
- A product will be used less if patients generally report problems or treatment failures.
- Doctors tend to make generalizations about drugs based on a few key experiences.
- We may not always be aware of our good or bad experiences... it may take some reflection, and that's where you come in! Don't be afraid to ask me to monitor specifically how patients do on your drug and give you feedback.

*chapter*

# 5 Tactics of Top Performing Reps

Sales can be an uphill battle. You can make as many as 12 calls that are "busts" (such as not getting to the customer or not getting quality time) before you get a productive call in. But don't get discouraged. Bad calls are an expected part of the job. And you were chosen for this job because you have the ability to shake off the minor disappointments and hit the last office of the day with the same enthusiasm as the first.

You need to be prepared to make every call a great one. In fact, the average doctor will see over 6 reps a week, and the number is just over 10 if you're talking about primary care doctors only. Once you get the doc's attention, you get a good deal of time — in fact surveys show the doc will spend approximately eight minutes with a rep once they get in the door.[1]

So what are the ways top reps make the most of their calls? How do they prepare to make every call meaningful?

---

[1] (Figures based on my 1997 survey of physicians, 62% in primary care, 38% in specialties.)

They do the following, and you can too:

1. Keep a file on each of your docs (or at least some notes). You should have some data on hand regarding each of your customers, and it should include not only details about the type of practice and patients seen, but personal data too. This will help you to stay on top of the customer's needs, and further develop a relationship. Here's a typical note card:

   Dr. Farah:
   - General adult psychiatry
   - Likes to focus on hospital practice and treatment resistant patients. Gets lots of referrals for chronic pain patients.
   - Reads the journal "Convulsive Therapy" about ECT
   - Personal — Always tries to sell me his books. Have to buy one to shut him up.
   - During the latest detail — he asked if dose needed to be lowered in renal impaired patients.

2. Take notes after important details. Why bother? Because your recall of the meeting will diminish after a day or two and you'll want some continuity from call to call. After a good call, reflect on why it went well. Can it be duplicated with that doc? Another doc?

3. Take notes after a bad call. Why did it go poorly? I know the temptation is to forget about the bad calls, but it can be very helpful to reflect on them. Reflection can make you see things in a different light. Many of you who played sports in high school or college will recall hours spent looking at films of games you lost. You analyzed the mistakes so you wouldn't make them again.

4. Note any journals the doc reads. Any articles on your drug in them?

5. Keep phone numbers handy that you use for product support. I once treated a lady with severe depression who was on an experimental drug for hepatitis (which was actually the cause of the depression). I was fortunate enough to see one of my best reps in the waiting room as I took her back to the office, so when I thought of an antidepressant for her, I simply popped my head out of the office and asked him "Kerry, is your drug safe with this new anti-viral drug?" He got on his cell phone and spoke to his medical information staff instantly and — "yes" was the answer.

That's service. The patient improved, I had my fears reduced about drug interactions, and the rep made it happen. But that was not luck. It was smart planning. Kerry has a list of numbers he carries, a cell phone, and a ready attitude. He plans and he delivers.

You'll read more about him in Chapter 18.

6. Stay interested in your own detail. When you have to deliver the same message hundreds of times in a year, it can get pretty boring for you. I have a good friend in the music industry who tells me that one of the hardest tasks he has is finding musicians for his concert tours. There are plenty of outstanding musicians, in fact, music schools put them out year after year and they all need jobs. But his challenge is finding someone who can play the same song night after night in one city after another, and make it sound like they are having the time of their life. Detailing is a lot like that. You have to educate physicians with your message over and over and never lose your enthusiasm for the product, Remember, if you are passionate about your message, we will be engaged, and if you are bored with your message, we will be bored as well.

7. Remember the personal touch. You are used to giving away various promotional items and sometimes even small "thank you" gifts. But

always take the extra step to personalize a give away item. A nice pen left on a desk is fine, but a day later it's just a nice pen. One with a card or note thanking me for my support will make an impact. We really do appreciate all the little things that make the day a bit brighter and help us keep the product in mind, but the top reps know their docs' personal preferences and make the most of them.

**Summary of Main Points:**

- Study your customers, just as you study your product.
- Study and reflect on your good calls and bad ones.
- Know your resources, they are also your customer's resources.
- Stay enthusiastic about your message.
- Always personalize your promotional activities.

# *Part II*

# *The Psychology of Prescription Habits and the Art of Medical Selling*

*chapter*

# 6 The Relationship and its Dilemmas:

## The Catch

In this book and in the introductory text *The Doctor as Customer*, I have used a great deal of ink (and you have spent a great deal of your time in the field) developing this concept: SELLING IS BASED ON RELATIONSHIPS.

But there is a catch.

Remember the catch in *Catch 22*? The bombardier wanted to be discharged from the air force due to insanity, because he didn't want to fly any more missions in World War II. But his doctor told him about the "catch" — which is, that he's not insane for wanting out of a war, in fact, wanting *in* a war is insane. Thus, his request for an insanity discharge was proof that he was really quite sane. That's some catch...

Your catch goes like this: you have to build a relationship in order to sell, but after a point the relationship becomes more and more friendly. And mixing business with friendship is tricky. As you become friends with your docs, professional barriers break down, talk becomes more casual and it becomes harder and harder to actually do the selling part of your job. Perhaps you've experienced this: you go to see a doc whom you would consider a friend, or at least the relationship has progressed beyond the usual "rep details doc," and you pull out a marketing piece or a research paper — what does the doc say? "Oh _______ (your name here), don't show me that! Tell me how the game was last night!" or "tell me about how your baby is doing!" In fact, tell me "anything but that marketing stuff." Now what do you do? You've built a great relationship, but it has become so personal that you can no longer be effective on the business side of the equation.

Because many of you are likely in this situation already with at least one of your doctors, here are some tips on how to handle this once it has occurred:

1. Change the focus of your detail so that it is very specific to that doctor's needs. If you know me well, you can detail on a level beyond the latest marketing emphasis. For example, a rep recently helped me find out if his product was safe with a new drug for Parkinson's disease (I had a patient enrolled in a Parkinson's study and she was severely depressed). This kind of specific help is where the level of the detail needs to be: the rep is a partner in patient care, not just someone who brings samples and tries to catch a signature. Use your excellent knowledge of your friend's practice to enhance the care of the patients.

2. Detail the impersonal by making it personal. For example, a friend of mine who happens to be a rep came by with these marching orders: "show Dr. Farah this marketing piece." Now I really wasn't interested in it, I

really wanted to know how her pregnancy was going and see the ultrasound shots of the little guy. I was thinking on a personal level altogether. The best approach here is NOT "let me go through this marketing piece," rather "please look at this with me, this is our new marketing piece, tell me what you think, doctor, what parts should I emphasize during my calls?" Get it? I'm still a friend, I am just asked as a friend to help with the presentation of the piece. The effect is still the same, the doctor sees the piece, but this scenario is better. I actually reflect on the piece with you, so I'm getting much more information out of it.

## *Avoiding The Catch*

So, how can you avoid the relationship that's "too friendly?" What steps can you take to prevent a slide down this slippery slope?

**Follow these simple rules:**

1. Allow others to talk to you about family or personal matters, but share much less about yourself. Professionalism is all about boundaries. Once they erode, and professional talk is personal talk, it is very difficult to back track and be business-like again in the future. An extreme example is the family business, which should be an oxymoron. It's a set up for disaster, you say things to family you'd never say to a business

partner and visa versa. Ever tried to work with your father or mother? You get the idea.

2. Keep the "professional speak" up as long as others are around, and then some. A good rule to follow is you never know who is listening. Now I don't want you to be paranoid, but if you want to joke with me, don't do it front of patients or staff. If the professional barrier has broken down between us, it could compromise the barriers I work to maintain with others.

   I was invited to speak out of state recently on behalf of an antidepressant. One of the reps who invited me shook my hand when I arrived, and we were seated across from each other at the table. He had spoken with my staff, but we had never met before that night, and he kept calling me "Andy."

   "So Andy, how was your flight? ...So Andy, you've got some spinach in your teeth..." Even if the docs ask to be addressed by first name, don't let the professional barriers break down in front of others — keep it "Dr." across the table of strangers.

3. Respect the same boundaries with the staff — no matter how friendly you get with them. Again,

you never know who is around to hear your "private" jokes. The same rules apply with the staff as with the docs. When you are the visitor in an office, you're really on unfamiliar turf and you don't know who is where. In fact, in our office, patients come from three different areas to approach the reception windows. It is a good rule to just assume that things are never what they seem. One of my Dad's favorite sayings is "every shut eye ain't sleep, and every goodbye ain't gone..." Indeed...

4. Don't trash the competition. The real message behind this is you lack respect for the work and products of others. That means we will lose respect for you and your message. Also, remember that most likely I use a variety of products and all but one of them in your particular class are your competition. So I have a pretty good understanding of how they work and how effective they are. Trashing the competition means trashing my treatment decisions for the patients on those drugs. More on talking trash in Chapter 6.

5. Talk less than your customer. Remember the movies *High Plains Drifter;* or *Hang 'em High*? Or even the *Dirty Harry* genre? Why does Clint Eastwood say so little in these movies? Easy... he

doesn't have to. Which is more effective? "Listen here, Punk, you better not go for that gun or I'll shoot you, so you better just stand up and put your hands in the air or you'll be sorry!" or "Go ahead, make my day..." Yes, sometimes the less you say, the more you say.

## *Great Relationship, But No Product Use!*

Now for the really tough question: What if you have a great relationship, but the doc still uses none of your product?

This can be one of the most frustrating aspects of your job. You build a relationship of trust and professional friendship, but the doctor is still not on board. And to make matters worse, you don't know how to ask the customer, your friend, "why?"

The simplest explanation is that the doc is just not comfortable using the product. Don't be afraid to ask this directly. If a doc is unsure of the exact dosing for example, they will avoid prescribing the drug. A problem like this is easy to fix, but it can still be standing in the way of product use if you don't ask. If it is a simple issue, such as correct dosing, we may be too embarrassed to ask! You may fear you'll insult us by talking about the basics. But if I'm not in a comfort zone with your product, tactfully explore why and let me know the facts.

It could be that a patient had a bad experience with the drug and the doc hasn't told you about it. In this case, it is probably OK to ask, "any problems with my product?" If one has arisen so severe as to limit use, then it is probably a rare reaction. See Chapter 3 for more on this problem.

Or it could mean that they just don't yet believe in the product. This is the most difficult position to sell from, even with a great relationship. Here's an example from my practice:

There is one particular product I rarely use. In fact, I wonder why they keep detailing me. I tried the product when it first came out, giving it to 20 patients, and keeping track of them carefully. None responded and most had side effects — so I gave up on it. The company is great and the reps are excellent, so I asked them, "how do you approach a doc like me, you tell me over and over the drug works great, and I tell you my personal experience indicates that I should stick to a product that I know will work and that I believe in?" As a result of this conversation, two ideas came up that you can use.

1. The first rep said "Dr. Farah, I know you don't believe in our product, but what if I take you to dinner with a doc who uses it a great deal and really likes it — he can tell you more than I can." What a great idea! I was ready to have dinner as planned, until I found out which doctor he was referring to — unfortunately, this doctor is more famous for Medicare fraud than treating patients wisely... which of course confirmed my suspicions about the drug... But still, it was a

great idea! You should use it, but it's a good idea to ask the doc in question whose opinion they respect before you firm up the plans...

2. The second rep's answer was also a great one: "I just want to keep the product in your mind, and hopefully you'll see some opportunity for its use, no matter how limited, and if that's how you find it helps your patients, then that's the role it will have." Great answer! This lets me know he respects my decisions, but still believes in the drug himself He also realized that rep service is really about what is best for the patient.

Sometimes, nothing will seem to work and the physician still does not use your drug. In that case, maybe the best thing to do is just maintain a presence for this doc. Continue to visit and drop off samples or information. DON'T get frustrated, and if you do, DON'T let the frustration show in the detail! Remain a friendly, calm presence, because you never know when your message and hard work will be boosted by some outside force (another doc's recommendation, an article, or a speaker program) that will tip the scales in your drug's favor. As always, the relationship will be the key.

## Summary of Main Points:

**To prevent a relationship that's "too friendly":**

- Respect professional boundaries at all times.
- Talk less than the customer.
- Remember that you never know who is listening! (patients around the corner? Staff down the hall?)
- Don't trash the competition.
- Know the staff as well as the docs.

**To rescue your sales from a "too friendly" relationship:**

- Personalize the detail to be very doctor specific — if you know their practice well then use that knowledge any way it fits into a detail.
- Engage the customer as your agent in education — review your product support materials together, don't merely present them.

**When sales are nowhere to be found despite a great relationship:**

- Don't give up hope, keep on seeing and detailing. Be a constant and confident presence.
- Bring in an outside expert to help you.
- And don't let your business issues become part of the detail.

## *The Last Word:*

Only once in my career have I told a rep that I would not see him. Actually, I was a bit of a coward about it and had our secretary do the dirty work for me. It was an unpleasant task, but I needed to do it, or rather, have someone do it for me... *Now*, I'm the most rep-friendly doc you'll ever meet, I try to sell books to reps as soon as they come in. But this guy was frustrated that I didn't use his product and that was all I heard about — his frustration. He spent no time telling me about his drug, just about how I was "hurting his numbers" and how he had made "no progress in the territory" and so on. Maybe it was cathartic for him, but that kind of information did nothing for my patients.

So, remember, if you are frustrated, rise above it, and don't let it get the better of you!

*chapter*

# 7 The Psychology of Prescription Choices

It's time to discuss the moment of truth: your customer picks up the prescription pad. At this point, you hope he or she is thinking of your product — and why it's the right one for the patient. So let's get to the heart of the matter:

What are the other influences apart from personal experience?

What is the prescriber thinking at the very moment the pen hits the pad?

Why one drug over another?

What about my drug?

Here are some key insights:

**1. The prescription based on a patient profile:**

A favorite rep recently asked me, "Dr. Farah, what patient profile makes you choose our antidepressant?"

I told her, "Anyone with depression," explaining that I believed many people could benefit from their antidepressant, not only those who fit a particular "profile."

This brief exchange touches on both the advantage and disadvantage of marketing a drug for a particular type of patient: on one hand, a doctor may immediately associate your product with the profile you've detailed. On the other, why pigeon-hole your product to just one type of patient when so many others could benefit? Whether you believe this strategy is advantageous to your product or not, describing patient types best suited for a drug's effects (and yes, even side effects) continues to be a main marketing strategy.

And because this strategy is based on what symptoms the patient reports, this can influence prescription patterns very early on in the decision making process. For example, as a patient tells us the history of their illness, they are really listing symptoms. When a cluster emerges that reminds us of the "right profile," we are often already thinking of the product even before the diagnosis is confirmed!

A patient recently came to me and said "I can't sleep, I've lost 12 pounds in two months because I can't eat, and I'm nervous..." After only one sentence from the patient, I was already thinking of one particular antidepressant, (mirtazapine, which if dosed low will cause sedation and stimulate appetite).

**2. Positive and negative "tags" influencing product choice:**

You are armed with positive tags about your product, and some of you are armed with negative tags about the competition's products. An example of a positive tag is "our product has no drug interactions" or "our drug is given once a day." An example of a negative tag is "our competition's drug is dosed three times a day" or "their drug interacts with Chinese food, causing the patient to spontaneously combust." (More on *untrue* negative tags in Chapter 16.)

This type of selling is usually tied to your marketing focus, and to some extent the marketing of the other products in your class. Positive and negative tags on products can help determine many prescription choices. In fact, one of the main ways doctors now choose antidepressants is by thinking about their side effects! Let me show you how this works — when I look at the list of all the antidepressants on the market and know *all* are theoretically effective for depression (and there are over 20 to choose from), obviously I look for reasons to pick one over another, and thereby I can narrow the list somewhat. For example, if I consider once a day dosing, that narrows it down to about 18 or so. So that tag threw a couple off the list. If I consider products that have minimal drug interactions, I'm down to five or so, and if I then look for those that lack sexual side effects, then I'm down to two! My choice is made by process of elimination. Now I can tell the patient "We are going to give you drug X because you only take it once a day, it will not interact with your other medications and will not change your love life."

The "positive tags" that come to mind were most often planted by the reps who called on me.

However, a negative characteristic is tagged on a drug by the competition. Those negative tags are often hyped out of proportion by competing reps. I can recall having picked up the prescription pad and thinking "drug X causes sedation... won't use that, drug Y has to be given 3 times a day... drug Z has a lot of potential interactions..." and narrowed the list by remembering the negative tags *whether or not I had ever seen those problems myself!*

Of course the patient may or may not experience the positive effects we hope to see, and may have a negative experience despite efforts to avoid problems through careful drug selection. There are no guarantees, only percentages of patients who experience one thing or another. Yet, the process is what's important - a busy doctor tries to quickly narrow a big list of drugs that may help, and positive and negative tags are often the way this is achieved. I can think of at least two positive tags for every antidepressant currently detailed at my office, and at least one negative tag planted by the respective competitors!

**3. Prescribing based on an "overriding principle":**

This is another way doctors may choose one particular product over all others at the moment of truth — they believe in one guiding principle that influences the choice every time. I recently interviewed a series of neurologists for a program on how doctors treat Parkinson's disease. Most (80%) "always prescribed" drug Z because they told me "it is neuro-protective." I asked what they would do if the patient simply failed to show clinical improvement on that particular medication, and all of them said they would tell the patient to continue the drug anyway. I mentioned the cost (as most patients with Parkinson's disease do not get medications paid for through Medicare), and most said they would sample it or tell the patient it was worth the price. The majority believed that they were prescribing a medicine that was preventing further demise in their patients. Obviously preventative medicine is good medicine, and they believe *that* principle should override any other in treating Parkinson's.

Another example involves a psychiatrist I know who always uses "atypical" antipsychotics first, because, as she puts it, "I don't want to be the one who gives the patient tardive dyskinesia" (a disfiguring movement disorder caused by long term exposure to "typical" antipsychotics).

Since some doctors will match a drug to an illness because of a belief that overrides any other concern, your challenge is to find out what that principle is, and then see if it applies to your product.

**4. Prescribing based on illness-specific characteristics:**

All illnesses have a variety of presentations, and some specific traits will lead a doctor to think of a particular product. This is different from the "positive tag" influence, because we are talking about the illness, not the drug. For example, many patients with Bipolar illness (manic-depressive illness) are categorized as "rapid cyclers." These patients can drastically change their moods in mere hours — sometimes they will experience several different mood states in one day (rage, mania, irritability, depression... I know some of you are reminded right about now, of that person you once divorced). There are several mood stabilizers I choose from to treat these patients, but I always think of one particular drug because it has been proven to be the best choice for rapid cyclers. This is especially important to me because these patients are so difficult to treat (studies show when a patient is hospitalized for bipolar illness with rapid cycles, less than 40% of them are well after eight weeks of treatment! And remember the patient from Chapter 1, who sang continuously? She was a rapid cycler.)

**The Psychology of Prescription Choices:**

- Doctors often choose a drug based on a patient profile.
- Doctors may also choose drugs based on positive attributes, or "tags" that are associated with the drug.
- Doctors will get the positive tags about your product from you.
- Doctors may rule out choosing a drug because of a negative tag, and negative tags about your drug come from your competition. And they don't have to be true to impact prescribing patterns!
- Some docs may prescribe certain drugs based on an overriding principle.
- Some may focus on aspects of the illness itself to guide their choice.

"For the hundredth time in as many days,
I don't want a free pen!"

*chapter*

# Selling to Different Physician Specialties

*Every customer is different.* This cliché must have been invented by a rep.

Here are some insights on the customer types you detail:

## The Internist and the Family Practitioner:

**Profile:**

It is no secret that these doctors are overworked and underpaid. The current pressures from managed care and HMOs forces them to do much of the specialty care needed by their patients — they are expected to be the cardiologist, psychiatrist, gynecologist... you name it. And, they are often discouraged from referring to specialists.

They will be time pressured, and rely heavily on staff members in the office to control their schedules and access to them. When we examine their prescribing patterns, we find that 70% are "non-spreaders" — which means they use two or three drugs in a category. If those fail to have the desired effect, then they are outside their zone of comfort, and will then refer to the specialist. Your goal is to help position your product as the number one or two choice in its category.

**The best way to detail them:**

- They are looking for the basics — remember the HITEC model.
- Cost concerns are important to them.
- Keep the message simple. They are time pressured and need to know the facts, and fast.
- Talk about the advantages to *them*, i.e., their life will be easier if they use your product. That means highlighting advantages such as ease of dosing for better patient compliance, or a low side effect profile for fewer complications.

**Strategies that don't work:**

- Don't "nit-pick" — they see the big picture, in fact, the total family. They get irritated when others lose sight of the forest by picking apart the trees.
- Don't give them the "high pressure" sale or the hard close. When surveyed, only pediatricians respond more negatively to this approach.
- Don't tell them you know their prescription data. Some must be protected from their naïveté. And when surveyed about this issue, responses in primary care were either negative or indifferent — but never positive. Also, all medical practices

are subject to various types of monitoring from insurance companies, and even audited at random by Medicare, so it's a particularly bad time to let folks know that you too, are watching them.

## *The Medical Specialist*

**Profile:**

Specialists include the cardiologist, gastroenterologist, pulmonologist (lung doc), oncologist (cancer doc), and nephrologist (kidney doc) to name a few. These doctors completed an internal medicine residency, and then completed further training in a specialized area. They set the trends in prescription patterns that primary care physicians follow. Remember the "spreaders" and "nonspreaders" discussed under primary care physicians? The prescription patterns of these doctors are just the opposite: 70% spread their choices among many options in a category, while only 30% stick to two or three favorites.

When it comes to challenging their prescription patterns, their responses on surveys were mixed. They didn't mind if they felt the rep was educating them or essentially telling them something new, but overall didn't desire a confrontational detail.

**The Best Way to Detail Them:**

- Above all, find out and target their special interests. They are specialized because they enjoy a particular branch of medicine. Find their passions and talk about them.

- Talk about the details, such as a drug's mechanism of action. They usually enjoy teaching as well, so take advantage of your time by asking them for clinical insights about your product.
- See if they are interested in community based research. Nearly all did some research as part of their fellowships, and they already know how to conduct a study. Researchers will become experts on a drug.

**Strategies that don't work:**

- Detailing at a very basic level (for obvious reasons).
- Glossing over study data can also be a mistake. Specialists tend to look at studies in more detail, and enjoy drawing their own conclusions.
- Avoid confrontation and challenging statements.

## *The Neurologist*

**Profile:**

Neurologists have a wealth of clinical knowledge. As they manage neurological patients, they will practice plenty of internal medicine and psychiatry along the way. They are also know as very reasoned in their clinical approach, and very often compulsive. Most order tests, and when those results come in, they tend to order more tests, and then sometimes order more tests...

They are a thorough and hard working bunch (of course, all physicians generally are, but these folks sleep less than the rest of us). If someone has a stroke in the middle of the night, they are the consultant who goes to the ER to see them. They have a very broad understanding of many medications.

**The best way to detail them:**

- Get an above average feel for their practices. You should explore every customer's experience with your drug, but these doctors can tell you a lot about how it fits their clinical needs.
- Hone in on special topics of interest such as sleep disorders, reflex sympathetic dystrophy, or temporal lobe epilepsy. They, above all specialties, seem to have passions for treating particular illnesses.
- They like detail in their details. Talk about things like mechanism of action, or new combination drug therapies. As a group, they are well versed on the basics, so take it a step further and hit the more complex issues.

**Strategies that don't work:**

- Absolutes: Try not to say "one drug fits all."
- Not appreciating the complexity of their approaches. Neurologists often see desperate people with desperate illnesses. Chronic

disabling conditions like pain syndromes that hurt 24 hours a day, or degenerative diseases that make one waste away until death. These illnesses make people beg for any relief. Fine doctors try all sorts of approaches (from magnets sewn into socks to reduce chronic diabetic neuropathy pain, to giving a patient two different antidepressants to keep away migraine headaches). It may be difficult to always understand their approaches from a snapshot view. Explore where your product helps in the severest of cases, and discuss its safety with other agents.

## *The Pediatrician*

**Profile:**

In medicine, you learn quickly that you must consider children as physiologically different from adults, and that's the main reason it takes a specialist to treat them. They are also well versed in many specialty areas. Despite traditionally low pay, they usually love what they do. Interestingly, when I've interviewed them (for consultations on how to detail them for various companies), I've found that they generally dislike the business aspects of practicing medicine more than all other specialties.

**The best way to detail them:**

- Cover safety issues! When surveyed or interviewed, the majority report patient safety as their main concern. This makes sense if you think about the responsibility they have. An adult can tell you they had a reaction or problem with a medicine much better than a one-year old. Cover doses and potential drug interactions thoroughly.

- They tend to use more product support materials (those that are designed for patients) than other specialties. Any product information you have, they want you to leave plenty of it!

**Strategies that don't work:**

- They don't like confrontation. You can't use any challenging or confrontational selling strategies. Remember, they have the stress of the patient care plus the patient's parents to deal with. Be the rep who recognizes this and you'll get results.
- Not respecting their time. Best to let them control the agenda and determine how much time is given for detail vs. small talk.

## *The Psychiatrist*

**Profile:**

Like all specialists, we set the prescription trends that others tend to follow. There is a wide pay range, because a higher percentage of psychiatrists choose to work part time when compared to other specialties. Also similar to other specialists, most are non-spreaders, and prescribe a variety of products. Combination medication therapy is currently in vogue in our field (but this approach goes in and out of favor every five years or so). Don't be intimidated by calling on a psychiatrist. The majority really enjoy rep visits, and are very focused on developing a relationship with you.

This is an exciting time to practice psychiatry, thanks to your industry, we have more agents available for the mentally ill than ever before. During some visits, don't be surprised if you get more questions about your pipeline than current products!

**The best way to sell a psychiatrist:**

- See us as managers of chronic problems. We deal with illnesses that are often life long and have many ups and downs (even in the literal sense, such as manic-depressive illness). So we are not looking for quick fixes or easy cures, there are few of those in our business. Approach your detail armed with issues related to the chronic nature of illness and long term strategies that are helpful for patients. Data about withdrawal syndromes, drop out rates, or findings that a product improves quality of life are good examples.
- Overall, pretty responsive to dinner programs or CME meetings.
- Relationships matter! Work on the relationship first, and you'll see great results.

**Strategies that don't work:**

- "Absolutes" do not sell us. I have seen unusual combinations of meds stabilize very troubled patients, and have devised great theories of why I pick certain drugs that should work, only to watch them fail miserably. When someone says "this is the best drug..." or "this always works for disease X," we begin to tune out.
- Avoid confrontation. Like pediatricians, most dislike this selling style.
- Sloppy use of language. Now, all of you reps are well spoken, and know your facts, but a psychiatrist is a professional listener. So, be precise in your language, and if you're unsure of a piece of data, tell us you'll look it up and get back to us rather than misstate it.

"And this drug is for social phobia..."

*chapter*

# 9 The Comfort Zone

As a resident, I was assigned marital therapy sessions with a couple that seemed quite miserable. They had no problem identifying their problems with communication: he would get angry about something, and get quiet. Then she got angry because he was so quiet, and she got louder, then he would explode in a rage. They would then ignore each other for a week until the whole process started all over again!

With the help of the clinic supervisors, I was able to outline a series of steps they could take to change the situation. The only problem was, they just didn't do it. Week after week, they came in and said they simply had not done what I recommended. The sessions were a nightmare. The husband ranted and raved, while the wife sat grinning, I assume at how foolishly her husband was acting, and every five minutes or so, she would wink at me... (I don't know why, but thank God the sessions were videotaped!)

My supervisor concluded that they were "comfortably uncomfortable." What a great phrase — they were uncomfortable all right, but it was all they knew, and they were unfortunately very comfortable with it. They were only uncomfortable with the prospect of change. You may even know couples like this (and I pray that you are not in a relationship like this).

Now, remember this couple when you see a doctor prescribe an older medication, a less efficacious one, or a poorly tolerated agent when compared to your drug. Because as lousy as one of those alternatives is for the patient, that doctor is comfortable with it. For example, I am a pretty well-read shrink. I search Medline several times a month and review articles for publication in various journals. But I don't know much about cardiology. If a patient on my inpatient service has high blood pressure, I prescribe generic clonidine. Many of you who detail some of the excellent new antihypertensive agents are shrieking in terror right about now.

But none of you are able to call on and educate psychiatrists about drugs like Norvasc, or Cozaar, and I am comfortable with the outdated option I learned as a resident. Obviously I can name a few of the new agents, but I don't know how to prescribe them. Also, think one step further — if I use a new agent improperly, I've got a lot of trouble on my hands. All doctors are comfortable treating some degree of hypertension, but hyPOtension, well... you get the idea.

One of the most important concepts in this book is: **prescriptions are written from a zone of comfort.** If you want me to use your drug, I have to be comfortable using it. That means:

1. **I need adequate knowledge on how to use it.**
2. **I need to know what problems to look out for, and what to do if they arise** — (see Chapter 2 about the HITEC model).
3. **I need to see that using it will be a positive experience for me and the patient.**

If a doc is *not* using your drug, it is because one of the three points above prevent them from being comfortable with it, and your challenge is to move that doc into the zone of comfort.

The first step is adequate knowledge. That means the HITEC model of detailing, and remember, some docs may not speak up if they fear the question is so fundamental that they will sound silly asking it. I spoke at over 80 dinner programs or roundtables last year, and I answered a lot of basic questions. Many docs would say, "this is probably a dumb question..." before they asked all sorts of things — some were fundamental (like "do you dose it in the morning or nighttime?"), and some weren't ("how do I dose it in patients with renal failure"), but these were all questions that they had plenty of opportunity to ask their reps, but for reasons we'll never know, they didn't.

Many docs will avoid using a product because they fear a side effect will occur and they will not know what to do about it. Side effects are common, and will occur with any product. The challenge to the physician is how to handle them. Remember my example of the antihypertensive agent? I used an old product partly because I feared I'd dose the new one incorrectly and drop a patient's blood pressure. When and if a rep tells me that one of the newer agents "will not lower a normal or already low blood pressure..." my fears will go away, and I'll have an alternative to generic clonidine. (I know that clonidine can drop pressures if dosed too high, but the point is, I am comfortable dosing it so this won't happen.)

And finally, don't be afraid to highlight the positive experiences a doctor has with your drug. *This*, above all other influences will drive growth. So, when a doc says, "I put a patient on your drug and she was able to improve, in fact, she's now so healthy she runs a three-minute mile," your job should then be to ask questions about this case, and get the doctor talking and reflecting on the success. Too often we forget positive experiences, and only remember negative ones. But detailed reflection will enhance the memory of the experience.

## *Beyond the Comfort Zone*

My research dealing with a physician's level of comfort with a product led me to an interesting finding: once a doctor is comfortable with a product, they will quickly develop "a feel" for using it. This does not involve an ethics violation of the Hippocratic oath. But it is a subtle and elusive concept, so bear with me as I write like a psychiatrist.

A feel involves not only prescribing from a zone of comfort, but somehow knowing in advance that a drug will suit a particular patient's illness well. Doctors who treat children with attention deficit disorder with hyperactivity (ADHD) often describe meeting a child and just knowing which drug will help (mainly because they want to save on waiting room repairs).

You may even ask a doctor "do you have a feel for our drug yet?" Because it takes some experience with a product to anticipate who may do well, who may experience what side effects, or who may need a higher dose.

Let me elaborate with some real life examples. I prescribe hundreds of antidepressants a year, and this experience has given me a sense for who may respond to what drug. For example, when I see patients who need help with anger management and irritability (or even violent outbursts), I always think of fluoxetine first. Does it work every time? Of course not — but often enough, and quickly enough for those target symptoms that I just sense those patients will benefit. But this is more than patient profile prescribing, because it goes beyond a simple match of drug X for patient profile Y. I know *when* to expect a response, and when to raise the dose, and what target symptoms usually respond first. This feel makes me very confident using the product.

Early on after the release of venlafaxine, I had a session with one of my patients. He was somewhat better after a few weeks, but not cured. I struggled with the decision of whether to push the dose or not. Was it too early? Was he at a therapeutic dose already? I simply lacked extensive experience, and didn't have a feel for what to do. So, I devised a solution: "drug exchange thinking." It is really quite simple: I had the patient on venlafaxine, a drug that I had no feel for at the time. So, I asked myself "what if he were on 20 mg of paroxetine and presented in the same condition?" Paroxetine is a drug I have extensive experience with, so should I push the dose, or should I tell him to stay on the same amount and come back in a month? I decided that if he were on the drug I was more familiar with, I'd push the dose higher, so that's what I recommended with the venlafaxine (and he did recover).

This idea hit me when my brother and I traveled to Europe one summer. I took my dollars and got some British pounds. The trip in England was miserable. It rained (of course). When I was in London the Freud museum was closed and the young lady I had gone over there to see decided she'd rather see my brother... But I knew exactly how many dollars my British pounds were worth. When I phoned to change plans and fly to France, leaving my brother and his new friend back in Yorkshire, I was a bit confused as to how many pounds I needed to equal the Francs. (It seemed like a good idea, I mean, if I'm going to be treated rudely in Europe, I might as well be in Paris where I expect it.) The currency exchange was a bit difficult for a Yank. Dollars to pounds to francs was too difficult, with all the jet lag and scorned feelings thrown in. It was easier to compare dollars to francs.

And similarly, with drugs we need a reference point as well. For example, if I prescribe 100 mg of thioridazine, or 5 mg of thiothixene, I know that each of these drugs in those amounts are as potent as 2 mg of haloperidol. Haloperidol is my reference, or gold standard. So, the lesson here is twofold:

1. Never hesitate to compare your dose with that of a well know competitor. If we lack a reference, we may avoid the product or give up on it too soon, and...
2. Never trust British women.

**Summary of the Comfort Zone:**

- Docs need to be comfortable with your product to use it.
- Comfort means adequate knowledge, even of the potential side effects, and enough positive experience with the drug.
- Knowing what to do about side effects is just as important as knowing what they are.
- Once comfortable, we develop a feel for certain products, that is, we sense when and how well they will work.
- This feel is based on our collective knowledge and experience.
- If we lack a feel for your drug, introduce us to drug exchange thinking (i.e. "what would you do if it were drug X at that dose equivalency, doctor?").

*chapter*

# 10 The Close

In *The Godfather,* the following story is told: the singer (or the character who was supposed to represent Sinatra) wanted out of his contract with a band leader. So he asks the Godfather (Brando) to negotiate for him. Brando's man held a gun to this band leader's head and explained that either his brains or his signature would wind up on the paper. Now that's a close! But that approach is illegal except in certain parts of New York.

In most of the business world, a sale is closed with handshakes and a contract. Once the bottom lines are signed, you've closed the deal and you know right then and there what you have sold.

Unfortunately, the traditional "close" just doesn't work that well in a medical setting. In fact, the traditional business close can be a real disaster for you. Why such a strong warning? Because a "close" technically is when you ask for a commitment of future drug use; yet as a physician, I don't know what the future holds. A rep asked me once to put my "next 10 patients on drug X." But I had no idea what the next 10 patients would need.

OK then, lets narrow it down to "the next 10 patients with depression." This is still a difficult position to put the doctor in, because the assumption is that this one drug is a good fit for anyone with a particular disease, and further, it implies that my judgment about what the patient needs is not a factor. You can see how this could remind the doc of the daily clinical demands received from insurance companies.

There is another pitfall in giving directives this specific: what if the doc agrees, and puts 10 patients on the drug, and most do poorly? The poor outcomes could simply be a matter of random chance, but the impact will be profound. Not only will future use of your drug be undetectable, but you could catch an earful on your next visit.

Early on in my career as a psychiatrist, I was amazed at how many doctors and therapists would simply tell people what to do in their personal lives. I was never comfortable with this style, and I didn't think it wise or ethical. So I asked for some advice from a professor. He confirmed that we really shouldn't tell folks exactly what to do. Our job was to relieve depression, anxiety, even psychosis, in order to get someone to a state of mind were they could make their own decisions. He instructed "if you say to a patient 'leave your husband,' well, you can go on with *your* day and later that week you've probably forgotten all about that session. But they have to live with that decision the rest of their life, and it's really not your decision to make." He went on to warn "If you tell someone 'do x, y and z and then you will be fine...' and they come back and say 'I tried x, y and z, and it didn't work...' or they may never have really tried the advice, but still say it didn't work... Now what do you say? You have lost your credibility..." He was right. Someone can prove you wrong and you lose credibility simply because you gave them an opportunity to do so!

So imagine a doc saying "I tried that drug on 10 people and 4 couldn't tolerate it because of side effects and 5 didn't get well, and one had a rash." Is all that data really accurate? And if so, were the patients on other drugs that could have caused those problems? You'll never know, but now your job is much harder.

One other note about the "10 patients on drug X..." How many of those patients really have to do poorly before a negative impression is formed? Surprisingly few. Negative information makes a much stronger impact than positive. For example, I recently got two messages side by side on my desk. One patient called to say "tell Dr. Farah that I'm doing great since he switched my medication, thanks..." The second patient's message read "tell Dr. Farah to call me as soon as possible, I've got a rash all over my body and I itch terribly and I think its from drug X..." After a couple of weeks, I won't recall what medication the first patient is on, but I sure will remember the second patient's drug.

## *The Best Way to Close:*

Remember the zone of comfort? We hesitate to use products that we simply are not comfortable with. It may be as simple as confusion about dose or if it should be taken on an empty stomach. One of the main points you should take from this book is you want your drug "in the comfort zone" for every doctor. Therefore your close should reflect this. Here are some examples:

"Doctor, I hope you've heard enough now to be comfortable using drug X."

"Is there anything else I can tell you that would make you more comfortable trying drug X?"

"I hope I've answered all of your questions and you feel confident using drug X..."

You get the idea... but if you are someone who unfortunately has marching orders to say "use my drug on the next 20 people you spot walking outside your window," then here's the best way to make it work:

Make the close into a helpful exercise that you will check on. Say something like "I hope you try drug X in a few patients because I'd love to hear next time how it went for them." The real message here is "your opinions are valuable — I want to know YOUR experience with my product." The close really doesn't sound that different, but the shift in premise is profound: you're no longer saying "you owe me 10 patients... you need to help my business..." you are instead saying "because your input is invaluable, please educate me as to how my product helps your patients..."

## *Summary*

- The secret to a successful close is simply making sure your product has now moved into the comfort zone of hesitation free use.
- If your company tells you to ask for "the next 10 patients," then turn it into an educational exercise in which you seek input about future use of your drug.

## *The Last Word:*

I always leave my patients with the phrase, "If you have any trouble, call me." They know I'm available to them. It's a positive, affirming message to leave someone with. Try this approach as you close your visit. I always like knowing a rep is available for anything that may come up.

*chapter*

# 11 Making the Message Stick

As reps, you want your message to stick long after you leave the customer. You have a wealth of specialized medical knowledge that can help hundreds, maybe thousands of patients in your territory. But getting the word out is half the job. So, what steps can you take to insure that your message is a lasting one?

The two best ways for your docs to learn and remember new information are through:

1. Association.

   and

2. Interaction.

Learning through association means associating your detail message with another piece of memorable information. It works best when you can get the memorable detail from the doc, and link it to your message. It means changing the detail from "our product lacks significant drug interactions" to "tell me if any of your patients are on an anticonvulsant, because our drug will not change the blood levels of these drugs..." Interactive learning is when the doc actually participates in the detail (not as a listener, but a real participant). Again, it will be a simple change: no longer would you read a detail piece to a doc, but you ask the doc to read it with you, and give you *their* interpretations and insights. Interactive learning is the most powerful kind. If you simply lecture to people, their recall of information after 5 days is less than 10%! If you use visual aids, then you can bump recall to 30-40%, but real interaction can result in 90% recall.

Now, what if you try these strategies and the doctor is simply nodding along, but not really absorbing the information. They are not engaged in the detail, and you fear you're wasting your breath...

I've pondered this for some time, maybe a lifetime. When I was growing up, it seemed that everywhere our family went, people would come up to my father and greet him enthusiastically. They would go on and on chatting to him, and he would ask "how's your family?" or "how's work going..." and keep the conversation going while we waited. As soon as they left, he would turn to my mother and say 'Marilyn, *who* the heck was *that*?" (Of course, like all moms, she always knew). He was too polite to tell them that he didn't remember them. Whenever they had met before, their message just didn't stick with him.

You want your docs to be listening for real, not just humoring you, and you want them to remember the main points. So here are the "Papa BEAR Rules" of detailing the customer that may be just playing along. These rules can overcome this problem and make your message a lasting one.

- **B**: Keep the message **BRIEF**. Keep your detail focused on clinically useful information. The more complex your message, the less memorable it will be. For example, which part of this quote can you recite from memory? "Neither a borrower, nor a lender be..." or "For loan oft loses both itself and friend, and borrowing dulls the edge of husbandry..."

- **E**: Link the message to the customer's **EXPERIENCE**. Think about these two different detail messages: "Our drug works the fastest of any in its class," or "Can you tell me about any of your patients who reported their asthma attack cleared up within seconds of using our inhaler?"

- **A**: **AVOID** clichés. When you speak in clichés, people tune you out. Every rep tells me that their drug is "well tolerated," "has a good safety profile," or "proven efficacy." These standard phrases have lost their impact because they are so commonly tossed out. Even if a cliché is truest for your drug, think of a creative way to say it.

- **R**: **REPEAT** the important parts of the message. You may think repetition is unnecessary because you are dealing with a pretty sophisticated customer, but each customer is also time pressured and has a lot on their mind. I actually was detailed the day I'm writing this about a new sleep agent. The rep told me *three* times that it can be taken in the middle of the night with no hangover effect in the morning. I don't remember the approximate price, and I don't remember which insurance plans cover it (both of which she reviewed as well), but I told two patients today, "if you wake up after midnight and want to take another one of these capsules, go ahead..."

## *How to Make the Message Stick:*

- Associate the message with something memorable, preferably brought up by the doc themselves.
- Detail with interaction.
- If these fail, remember Papa BEAR's rules: Detail with a **Brief** message that draws on the doc's **Experience**, **Avoid** clichés, and conclude with a **Repetition** of the main message.

*chapter*

# 12

# *The Secrets to a Successful Speaker Program*

Why do speaker programs have the potential to greatly influence prescription habits? Because doctors will always learn medicine from other doctors. Medical education is based on hierarchical learning — students are taught by residents, who are taught by attending physicians. And when thrown out in the world of private practice to swim on your own, you must rely on visiting faculty and speaker programs to get the latest material. The dependence is magnified when one is looking for information outside his or her specialty. For example, when I lecture to internists on antidepressants, they are eager to get as much usable information as they can, and usually ask numerous questions. They practice plenty of psychiatry in primary care, and need the latest clinical information, so they really take advantage of my visits.

The speaker program, when successful, is a win-win-win situation. Your territory gets the latest information and the patients benefit, your speaker has enjoyed the business opportunity, and your return on investment should be evident after a couple of months of prescription data filter back.

Here are 8 guidelines that will insure your program is a success:

**1. Prepare your speaker:**

Why take the time to contact your speaker before the event? This speaker is a pro, right? Maybe so, but the goal of the program should be to meet *your* needs in *your* territory. I encourage reps to touch base with me or my assistant and let me know 1. who will be in the audience, 2. what information they want me to emphasize, and 3. any special concerns they have. For example, I recently was informed about the audience members who had "RSVP'd" for my talk on a new antidepressant: it consisted mostly of primary care physicians and neurologists, many had never used the product, and they were interested in my experience with the drug in our pain clinic. Also, the competition had spread untrue information about the drug being "unsafe at therapeutic doses." With this information, I was able to tailor a talk that met the territory's needs exactly.

If you contact a speaker, and find that unfortunately this doctor is not interested in hearing about your needs, then you're probably better off canceling them and getting a speaker who is.

**2. Control the program:**

You are the host or hostess, and this program is your event — so don't be afraid to take control! Let your guests know the agenda, especially when there is an event to follow. Also, do *not* hold up dinner until after the talk —

most people have worked all day, and if they sit there hungry they will soon become irritated at your speaker (who will seem particularly long winded if dinner is waiting), so they are not likely to absorb much information. It is best to let the waiters take the orders first, drop a first course, and then start the program. Eating is a silent affair, while ordering is a two way conversation.

You may find yourself in uncomfortable situations during your program and taking charge is imperative. For example, I spoke at an unusual program last year, it was in a tent at a zoo. No kidding, at a zoo. So all the doctors brought their children. Unfortunately, they behaved as if they were at, well, the zoo. They ran around, made plenty of noise, and played during my program. One even came up to the screen where my slides were projected, repeatedly, and played with it! The parents of Chuckie, Angelica, and Tommy let them roam free. The reps were at a loss. Should they have disciplined other people's children? After all, these were the doctors' kids! Obviously, the program was a disaster. I though about it during my long plane ride home. What should the reps have done? I concluded that a rep should have interrupted the talk and suggested the kids join them for a tour of the zoo... outside.

If your program is disrupted by a child-like physician, then you have another dilemma on your hands. The most common scenario is the audience member who makes speeches during the Q and A time, and those speeches are unfavorable toward your product. Usually, such an attendee has hit the open bar a bit heavy during the program. In this case it is best to let the speaker handle this, as we are either trained to handle it, or have learned from experience how to deal with disruption. If the speaker sits back and lets this go on, *then* you should take charge. It will require tact, but you have the skills. You need to interrupt the speech, and say "in the interest of time, let's move on to some other questions, and after the program, Dr. Blabbermouth, I'll be glad to give you the number for our medical science liaison, since you have many questions that we just can't cover with tonight's time constraints..." (There is at least one medical science liaison who has never forgiven me for offering her services to such a difficult doc...)

Remember that YOU are in charge. I see too many reps sit by and let a program fail to meet their needs (usually because they are simply being too polite) when a simple request will make a huge difference. You can still be polite, but don't be passive. If music is playing over the program, then ask the staff to turn it off. If attendees can't hear the speaker, ask him or her to speak up, or move to the center of a room. As I said, it's your program!

**3. Ask the questions that you want answered:**

I attended a recent talk entitled "All about Drug A" and the speaker (who should have been canceled if the rep knew about rule 1 above) delivered a talk "All about Drug X," which is a direct competitor to drug A. I felt bad for the sponsoring rep. But, he managed to make the best of it. He asked the speaker some questions about his product, and salvaged the program from total disaster. The information the rep wanted us to hear was nowhere to be found, until he asked about it.

**4. Introduce the speaker to the key people:**

What happens when you get the thought leaders in your community on board with your drug? It means other doctors copy their prescription patterns. I once asked a rep "Ben, I like you a lot, but why do you come to see me three times a week?" He confessed that when I write one script for his drug, it means seven more from primary care docs who look to our practice for guidance with unfamiliar drugs.

Speakers who network with the crowd can answer any specific questions individuals may have. Also, the information recall of the attendees will be greater if there is a personal connection with the speaker. One of the introductions I've used before talks involved showing some slides of my baby pictures. I've met people 4 years later who said "you're the guy who showed a picture of yourself in the tub when you were two years old!" Now that's what I call a personal connection...

**5. Use the trip:**

When you fly an expert in for a talk, take advantage of the opportunity that provides. If we are in town, then use us! I've flown into cities in time for a lunch talk, then some office visits, and a dinner program. Sometimes there have been breakfast programs the next morning before I leave. It's standard to pay the honorarium for the first talk at the usual fee, and each one after at a discount. But I shouldn't tell you that part. In fact, I was wrong. We get more pay with each subsequent talk.

**6. Personalize the invitation:**

Consider these three invitations:

"Dr. Perry, we are having Dr. Farah fly in tonight to talk about drug X, please come."

"Dr. Perry, you are the sexiest creature known to man, I can't contain myself, we must talk in public from now on, please come to our program tonight."

"Dr. Perry, you had asked me about the dosing of drug X in Obsessive Compulsive disorder, well, Dr. Farah will be here tonight, and he will cover that topic. I told him that we had a physician in our community (the sexiest creature known to man) who wanted to know the dosing schedule, so tonight you will hear it from the expert."

The first invitation is impersonal and gives Dr. Perry no inspiration to attend. The second will lead to the appointment of an independent counsel. The third is very personal, how can Dr. Perry say no?

**7. Invite the key prescribers:**

Obviously you need to get the main prescribers out to the program, and sometimes this means asking your speaker to help. If they are in town early enough, consider an office visit in which you take them to meet a key doc and see if there are any specific questions they hope the speaker will answer. This is combining the personalized invitation with the personal connection!

Too often though, a program is crashed by non-medical staff. A spouse or office manager is one thing, but in our community, the word is out, "don't invite the so-and-so clinic doctors, because every secretary and their three brothers will show up!" This one clinic is notorious for taking advantage of your generosity, which means a poor return on investment. In this situation, stress to the doctors that there is limited space, and you need an RSVP for their attendance. This problem is one of the reasons "dine and dash" and roundtable programs are gaining popularity, they target only the docs, and your resources are better spent. But it is a good rule to always say yes to spouses attending. When told not to bring them, many docs simply choose not to go. Your customers spend enough time away from family — and programs that include them are usually well attended.

**8. Have a back-up plan:**

I was setting up my slides one night before a program when I noticed a lot of smoke outside the window. I thought it was odd, since I was on the top floor of a 34 story building. I looked down to see the building next door going up in flames. After we were told to evacuate our building, four reps and I stood on a sidewalk watching the blaze. Now, these guys were pros, and within minutes they had a plan. Each camped at a strategic location, and caught the docs as they were headed into the area. They told them of the new restaurant we were going to use (which they had arranged on mobile phones) and we pulled off a successful program, only half an hour off schedule! One rep even managed to get on the 10 o'clock news! ("...tell us again how you rescued all those people from the inferno...")

This kind of disaster is a once in a lifetime occurrence, but are you prepared for the restaurant getting the date wrong, or a major traffic tie up that delays things two hours? Think about your territory and the problems you need to prepare for.

No matter how poorly you think you've done hosting a dinner program, there's always some story more tragic. A rep and I were sitting in the bar at an ocean-side restaurant waiting for my program to start. As the invited docs drifted in, he became puzzled." I don't recognize any of these folks," he said, "and where's my manager, she said she'd be here." So he called her on a cell phone. I could hear her ask "Where are you?!?" And yes, we were at the wrong restaurant. There was a medical program there that night, just not mine. But there is a happy ending, we made it to the right place in time, and we left our drinks on another company's tab.

## *One Last Tip:*

As a rep who arranges for lunches at offices in your territory, you are unfortunately dependent on others for that service — the caterers. Remember the line from *The Jerk* when Steve Martin mentions that "This is the best pizza in a cup I've had?" Well, you may have a situation like that if your caterer forgets the plates, and believe me, it has happened. Take out a little insurance, it will cost you about $5.00. Buy some paper plates, cups and plastic forks and throw them in your trunk. You may never need them, but they could save your life.

**Summary of Main Points:**

- Let your speaker know who is coming, and what they want to hear. A prepared speaker can meet your needs.
- Control your program!
- Ask questions you want covered.
- Network your speaker with the attendees, and especially the key prescribers.
- Make the most of the trip with as many programs as possible.
- Invite the top docs, and take measures to prevent party crashers.
- Always say yes to spouses attending.
- Improve your attendance using the personalized invitation.
- Have a back-up plan in case disaster strikes.

chapter

# 13 Getting Invited Back

My partners and I once arranged a meeting to get some business advice from a friend who is a chemical engineer. He had patented a chemical process that industries around the world needed to reduce their waste. He is a multimillionaire (possibly a billionaire, but I didn't ask). We found him wearing jeans and a T-shirt in the back of a chemical warehouse. We had bought Armani suits for the occasion but obviously found ourselves overdressed. I heard a great deal of good advice that day, but the main thing I remember was our friend holding up a vial of harmless byproduct he could create from toxic waste and saying, "you wouldn't believe how simple this is."

Sometimes the most valuable information is the simplest.

I was reminded of this lesson when a pharmaceutical company asked me to answer a very important question: **"How can our reps be sure that they will be invited back to any office?"**

So I did some research. I asked my partners to list which reps were welcome anytime, the ones that were always invited back. Then I asked members of our medical society the same thing. I wrote down all the names of the reps and products they represented. The ones I didn't know I called to chat with. No obvious pattern emerged, many different companies, many different products, and many different styles and marketing strategies.

But, not surprisingly, the same names kept showing up, from specialty to primary care offices. Once I interviewed these reps, the answer was simple — **they loved their jobs.** They all had fun every day. Just loving what you do and letting your passion for the job show was the key to an open invitation to any office. It was that simple.

My consultation was a bit more formally written, but it went something like this: if your representatives approach each call as an opportunity to enjoy themselves and have fun, the customers will have fun too, and then they will see you as a welcome break to the grind of the day, not a part of it.

But this is serious business! What if we are seen as flippant?

Well, not every doctor is Patch Adams, and not every rep should try to be a comedian, you can enjoy what you do and still be respectful and scientific. Use your own style to your advantage. I know a great rep who is usually all business in his approach. So, at first he seems a bit stiff, but one day he came into my office and I had the radio on to catch the news. I began cursing politicians and he joined in. Now I look forward to his visits, as we talk about 30% medicine, 70% politics.

The official study report didn't say "just have fun," but it was close! It read: "The representatives who were spontaneously mentioned, and scored 'always welcome in our office' were distinguished from their colleagues by bringing a high level of enthusiasm and genuine passion to their work. And, interestingly, doctors and their staffs also scored these representatives as 'genuinely concerned about patient welfare.' Thus, the overwhelming positive energy they brought to the workplace also sent a message to the physician customers that the reps viewed their work as a way of enhancing patient care. They accounted for approximately 15% of the individuals in the current sales forces operating in the territory studied."

"Representatives who were identified spontaneously and scored 'never see' or 'avoid seeing' were identified with comments such as 'too aggressive,' 'talks negatively about products from the competition,' 'intrusive,' 'poorly informed,' and thus brought negative energy to the encounters. They represented approximately 6% of the individuals in the current sales forces operating in the territory studied."

Aim high. Be in the top 15%.

# *Part III*

# *Strategies for The Tough Sells*

*chapter*

# 14 Pearls and Swine

*"Neither cast ye your pearls before swine. They will trample them underfoot at best..."* Matthew 7:7

We have all learned this lesson the hard way. My favorite illustration is from the movie *Animal House*. An English teacher stands before a class of disinterested freshmen. He tries to lecture on Milton, but soon realizes that the class is completely oblivious to his words. Finally he pleads, as the bell sounds and the animals scatter "...Look, I'm serious! This is my job!"

The lesson is clear — some physicians are not going to be receptive to your message. It can happen on any day and for reasons you may never be aware of. It is best to try the strategies discussed in Chapter 11 first (such as the Papa BEAR rules), but if you still have no impact, then back off the detail and mentally regroup. You can potentially do more harm than good by forcing the issue.

Here are a couple of real life examples: one of my partners, you'll recall by his affectionate title "the Script-Nazi," is notorious for being rude to reps. He's been practicing medicine for about ten years longer than I've been alive, and he's a bit stuck in his ways. He even tries to avoid eye contact with reps. One day, a rep, we'll call him Greg (and he says it's OK to use his name) managed to actually get an appointment with the Script-Nazi, who saw him sitting in the waiting room. He walked quickly by, and as he patted Greg on the shoulder said, "consider yourself seen..." End of appointment.

Another partner, Joe, was having a rough day. He had been on call the night before and didn't get much sleep. A rep was kind enough to bring us lunch, but also detailed us non-stop as we ate. Joe asked her to hold off on the detail for a minute while he cleared his head and relaxed. But she took this as a joke, and started again to run through her detail aids. After about 10 minutes, Joe decided that he had heard enough and went to his office to eat alone. The reps information was good, but she failed to read her audience — it was simply not a good time to be detailing Joe. In fact, there are no good times to detail Joe; that is, while he's in the office. He's the kind of customer who needs dinner programs or private meetings outside the chaos of the office.

Am I saying my partners are swine? Well, yes, I suppose I am. But we all have rough days, and we all have a little swine potential. When you see the pig, trust your instincts and save the pearls for another day.

I'm not pretending this is an easy task, but practice reading your audience, and tailor your message accordingly. I travel to lecture at numerous speaker programs each year, and I always appreciate an open bar before my talks. My jokes are much funnier (at least to me), and the audience is more receptive. Now, you can't bring alcohol to your lunches, but you can do the next best thing. I always ask the reps who host my programs to tell me about the docs that are there, what they like to hear about, and I ask for the names of a couple of people who can take a joke and I use their names in some of the humorous parts of the lecture. You can feel out the docs by talking to the office staff. A simple "Dr. Joe is having a rough day" overheard in a hallway should not go unnoticed.

Great customer service means you are probably the only person that will recognize I am having a bad day, and you react accordingly.

Only once was I too clever for my own good. I asked the rep before a dinner program for the name of a doc I could pick on. She told me Dr. John could use a laugh, so I told one of my routine jokes:

"John, over there, was telling me about his last trip to the beach. He had gone there to relax because he had just been through an awful divorce. Now, he was jogging on the beach one morning when he tripped over a bottle. As he picked it up, a Genie came out and said 'Dr. John, this is your lucky day, sort of. I'm supposed to give you three wishes, but you just signed this awful divorce agreement, and no matter what you wish for, your ex-wife gets twice as much.'

'Wow, three wishes, give me a million dollars!'

'Fine,' said the Genie, 'it's in your bank account, but your ex-wife just got 2 million... what's your second wish?'

'I sure like this beach, give me ten miles of beach-front property!'

'Done, but your ex just got 20 miles on the other side of the island...'

'So, she always gets twice as much as I get?'

'Right.'

'Then I tell you what Genie, for my last wish, just beat me half to death...'"

Afterwards, the rep came up to me. "I didn't know you were friends with Dr. John!" I explained that I had really never met him before tonight.

"...Then how did you know he just went through such a terrible divorce...?"

"No kidding... that's why I thought he needed a laugh..."

## *Swine Precautions:*

- If a doc has swine potential, then first check out how their day is going with the staff if possible.
- When it appears to be "a bad doc" day, try the Papa BEAR rules first.
- If there is still no impact, back off, and just let them know you see it is a bad time to detail, but you are available if they need anything.
- Remember, these guidelines are for GOOD docs having BAD days. For dealing with docs who always have bad days, well that's the next chapter...

## *The Last Word:*

If *you* are having the bad day, then take a break from detail visits, and make it a paperwork day. You can ruin months of work with one bad call! (If asked, I'll tell your manager you really did stop by.)

chapter

# 15 *Dealing with Difficult Customers*

I first began researching ways to help reps deal with difficult customers after I had lectured at a CME program last year. The hosting rep and I were chatting when a doctor (who showed up late and missed the talk) came over and said "This rep is always trying to sell me that junk Zoloft."

Now, you and I know that this doctor was wrong. Zoloft is a fine drug that has helped millions of people. Reps who sell any other antidepressant will say that. But this doctor's behavior provides an excellent opportunity to examine the whole process of the difficult customer.

In this example, the doctor has to be in control of the situation — he sees two people chatting — he's not included, so he makes himself the topic by simply acting rude.

Here's another typical situation: a rep told me, "I saw one of your former partners the other day, and it was the first time he actually spoke to me and was even friendly! He talked about my product and how he liked it, and then he had the nerve to ask me to pay for some private party he was throwing!" (No secret why he's a *former* partner!) I'm sure you are reminded of a few docs on your list who operate with the mentality "what are you going to do for me..."

These customers obviously fall under the category "the rude doc," but other specific customer types covered in this chapter are: the silent doc, the indifferent doc, the "sample hog," the "nitpick," and the "know-it-all's."

## *The Silent Type*

Sounds strange, but it occurs. And how can you hope to abide by the "talk 20% listen 80%" rule of sales if your customer is the silent type?

The rule of thumb is to **ask open ended questions** — that forces them to be more conversational. If you ask "Do you find our drug is easily tolerated by patients?" you are really posing a "yes or no" question. A simple change such as "What side effects do you see with our drug?" means they will have to list them (unless you are lucky enough to have a product for which the answer is "none"). Think about this strategy on your next call, and change your yes/no questions into open ended ones. You'll be surprised at the dialogue this will generate.

Another strategy involves **finding out what they really like to talk about**. If they spend five minutes talking about fishing, well, that's fine. They've just spent five minutes telling you more than they told the last rep. The key is simply getting them talking — about anything. Detailing will come later, but first you need dialogue. I was invited to "ride with the reps" on a speaking trip recently, and we stopped by to see a doctor who was notorious for never opening up with reps. The receptionist told us he had just gotten back from a reunion in France. I had heard he was about 70 years old, so when we met, I asked him. "Is there any chance you were in the Normandy Invasion?" We talked for a half an hour about his war experience. Patients were backed up, and he just kept talking. He thanked the rep for bringing me by, and for the first time asked for her card. Now she finally knows what he likes to talk about.

## *The Indifferent Customer*

Similar to the silent customer is the indifferent one. They may be quiet, or may not be. One can be fairly quiet and still have strong opinions, so don't let that fool you. The indifferent docs are a particular challenge, because they don't seem to care one way or another about the detail. They respond with generic comments like "sounds good," or "they're all good drugs in that class." Or they may be passively negative and say things like "I don't use it much..." or "I don't see a need for it in my practice." They don't give you an opening to discuss their reservations because they are expressed vaguely or not expressed at all.

First try to **determine their areas of special interest**. They may have a specialty area they enjoy greatly. I'm sure you remember the Script-Nazi from previous chapters. If a rep actually gets into a dialogue with him, on a good day he'll be indifferent. He'll say "sure, it's a good drug, they all are..." no matter what the detail is about. But if you ask him about attention deficit disorder, he'll deliver a lecture on the spot that starts with the phrase "70% of the population has ADD, the other 30% are very boring people!" (The exact figure is 10% of males, 1% of females, and 30% *of those* kids continue to exhibit symptoms past age 18 and have the adult form as well, but we're all a bit afraid to correct his statistics).

What if you find no areas of special interest? I would then ask them a question related to a typical "hot button." If you've ever done any TV or radio interviews, you quickly learn that the producers and reporters are not to be trusted. They will question you beforehand, and see what gets you worked up or even angry. For example, I once told the news crew that it would be inappropriate for me to comment on any specific case, but I could talk in general about mental illness. They all agreed, but as soon as the cameras were on I heard "Dr. Farah is here to explain how Mr. So and So was crazy enough to kill those people..." (My reply "I told you those types of questions were not appropriate..." — and the morning show audience got a boring lesson in psychiatric ethics regulations.)

Now, I don't think you need to ambush your customers just to get them talking, but there are some hot buttons in every field that no one is indifferent about. "What effect has managed care had on your practice?" "Do you think psychologists will be prescribing drugs soon?" "Is it true that anti-arrhythmics are harmful after heart attacks?" Pretty hot stuff...

## *The Rude Docs*

Unfortunately, one or more of your docs just came to mind. Let's examine why they are acting that way — in most cases, it is a way to be the center of attention or take control. Let's revisit the situation I described earlier in which the rep was promoting an antidepressant, and the doc says "Oh, that drug is junk..." There are three ways to handle this:

1. You can joke about it. One way to diffuse narcissism is to laugh at it.
2. Or you can put the rude person on the spot — bring in a third party to expose how absurd they are acting. The rep that day turned to me and said, "Dr. So and So here thinks our drug is junk, what about that!" I told him I was sorry he missed my presentation, and I shared some new data about the junk's efficacy in panic disorder. He was then in the ridiculous position of defending his rude statement to a member of the speakers' panel for the drug. But let's not lose sight of the goal, those first two maneuvers may diffuse the rudeness temporarily, but you are still in the position of selling a drug to a control freak. So you'll eventually want to get to #3:
3. Play the game. If control is so important to them, then let them have it. Ask them "How would you talk about my drug to the other doctors?" Actually ask them for advice. They get control,

and get to hear themselves talk (which is their goal anyway), and they are talking about your product.

## *The Nit-Pick*

One attending physician from my residency could recall the tiniest bits of minutia about medicines with his photographic memory. When a rep tried to detail him, he would say something like "what about the .05% risk of Stevens-Johnson skin reaction?" Obviously, he was just showing off the fact that he could remember an obscure statistic. But it puts the rep in a tough spot. Should you point out that he's being absurd? Probably not...

There are two main ways to deal with the nit-pick:

1. Redirect the focus of his comments to actual clinical practice: say something like — "tell me if you've seen obscure skin reactions in your patients on my drug." He will then confess that it has never happened. If *you're* the one to say "That's rare — less than a 1% chance — you're being a nit-pick Dr. Kramer," then you sound defensive. That will just perpetuate this non-productive dialogue. Your task is to instead let him realize the insignificance of his remark, and then steer the dialogue toward matters of patient care. OR
2. Go with the flow and humor him. If he wants to talk about obscure facts, well, fine, let him talk. Let this guy spend 10 minutes rambling about

your product. Don't get frustrated because your message isn't getting out, let him ramble, then look for openings to get your main detail points in.

"The doctor will see your insurance forms now..."

## *The Sample Hog*

Unfortunately, one or more of your docs just came to mind. These are the customers who ask for samples repeatedly (and may even call you at home demanding them) YET they rarely prescribe your product. They use your generosity to fund their own indigent program. I know one such doctor in our community. He actually had the nerve to send *his* patient to *my* office for samples — "Dr. P says he don't have no more Prozac but you might..." One of those fun waiting room situations...

It is reasonable to give a hog three months, in which you sample them heavily as they request. Three months allows for plenty of time to follow up with numerous patients, and see if the samples are effective and well tolerated. They will have formed an opinion about the drug by then. If the three months go by, and there is still no support of the product, then it is time to focus on other customers. I would talk to them like this: "Gee Dr. P., I'm glad your patients are benefiting from the product, and since many of them may need samples, perhaps some would do better on the indigent program." If you don't have an indigent program, I would tell them just that — "...we don't have an indigent program — but here are **the most cost effective ways to prescribe the product**."

You will also want to **depersonalize the situation**, that is speak in terms that are more "matter if fact" than personal. It may be likely that the sample hog tries to make it a personal issue ("That rep for drug X won't give me any more samples..."), as this can be a way to manipulate more free drugs from you, but you need to keep it all business: explain that these are the samples for your entire territory, and if one *office* (don't say doctor) gets a disproportionate amount, then other offices go without.

## *The Know-it-Alls*

I once heard a doc question a rep about "the effects of your drug on delta wave sleep patterns in the elderly..." Everyone present was aware that the drug was new, and no sleep studies related to it were available. But once again, let's focus on the process at work in this customer's head. We are dealing with a doctor who needs to feel smart, and he wants others to say, "wow, he knows about delta sleep waves..." The sales situation or the dinner program are seen to him as opportunities to stroke a giant ego.

The key to selling this doc is again, going with the flow and humoring him, but then go a step further: actually enlist him as your agent. This will be flattering and enable him to teach you. Again, get him talking, reflecting on the product. You actually say things like: "I'm glad you brought that up — you are the only expert I know on sleep medicine, and since there are no studies yet, perhaps you could share your beliefs about sleep stages and what effects drug X may have on them..." You'll be catching more flies with honey.

chapter

# 16 Answering the Critics

In the ruthless world of drug marketing, trashing the competition has unfortunately become more prevalent. There is nothing improper about highlighting the differences between your drug and those of the competition, but some reps may simply talk negatively about other products. If the negative comments turn out to be false or exaggerated, then this approach will ultimately damage the credibility of the rep making those statements and paradoxically help the sales of the drug being criticized, but in the short run, it can be harmful.

You may have already experienced being trashed by the competition. You may recall one day in which every doc you visited repeated the same false statement about your drug — such as "...the so-and-so rep told me your drug was the major component in the napalm dropped on children in Vietnam..." And you realize, while you've been out there doing an honest job, someone else has been out there spreading lies about your drug.

As Mark Twain said, "a lie can travel halfway around the world while the truth is putting on its shoes." But don't panic, because there are a few ways to make sure recovery is swift and sure.

1. Immediate reaction is important, therefore **don't be defensive**. You don't need to be the one who is defensive when a lie has been told. Instead, be self-assured, and remind us that the competition must be worried about your product if they have to resort to dishonest tactics, then tell us why it is untrue: "You see doctor, napalm was really a form of gasoline, while our drug is an antidepressant. They are quite different chemically. Here are some articles that show the difference between gasoline and serotonin reuptake inhibitors..."

2. **Get the facts out fast**. And get product support materials that state the facts in front of the doc. Lies work only if the person hearing them is uninformed.

3. **Prepare** to be trashed. Yes, as part of your game plan it will serve you well to be prepared. You can likely list right now at least one misstatement that has been made about each of your products over the past year. Do you have ready access to articles for support, and know the facts off the top of you head?

4. **Use this as an opportunity**. An opportunity to talk at length about your product, dispel the myths, and then to remind us how we've just been insulted. If a competitor of yours tries to influence customers with half truths and misinformation, they obviously don't think much of your mutual customers, nor the patients' needs. Medicine is serious business, and we need good data to base our decisions on, not deception.

Turn the trashing into an opportunity. Here's a real life example: One of the drugs I use quite often was recently trashed by the competition because "It can cause birth defects!" or, so they told me. I, in turn, told the reps the facts. The facts are: if you mega-dose poor little pregnant rats with this drug at nine times daily dosing, all the rat babies are just fine. If you then doudle-mega-dose the poor expecting rats at 18 times recommended daily dose, some of the little guys don't look so hot. But, it's probably because the mom rats were so drugged that they didn't eat well. Now, the next best comparison, interestingly, is from the drug company who was trashing my favorite, and it involved their drug at eight times dosing (a test dose lower than the drug they were trashing!). So, it's really not comparing apples with apples. It's simply bad selling to give pieces of data and then state conclusions. With the facts, one realizes that no such conclusions can be made about the drug's potential for birth defects in humans at therapeutic doses. Moral of the story: know your facts.

Ultimately, a single rep trashing the competition will make everyone's job harder. Your job is primarily one of education. False information puts doctors in a position of not knowing what to believe, and puts those of you taking the high road at a real disadvantage, because you spend your time defending, not detailing. So, take my advice, and just say no to talking trash.

## *The Last Word:*

"A man should be known by the enemies he keeps."
Ernest Hemingway
(letter to interviewer)

# *Part IV*

# *The Next Level*

"Good rep service means better patient care. The truth is, reps are really in the service industry, just patient service, with none of the praise. A rep should approach every call with this in mind."

Dr. Gregg Perry

chapter

# 17 Insights into the Complexity of Medicine

In the textbook version of medical practice, the doctor sees a patient, completes an evaluation, and decides on some form of treatment. We expect patients to be motivated toward wellness, and generally follow our advice and respond favorably. As obvious as this seems, it is not always true. But, as I said, that is the textbook version. When a patient does not respond to treatment or lacks a desire to get well, we need to know why. This chapter will explore the most complex aspect of your customer's job. You are about to gain insight into one of the greatest medical dilemmas, how to evaluate and treat patients who *don't* want to get well...

One of the most neglected areas of medical education and research is something called "somatization" — and a basic understanding of this area will set you apart from your colleagues and enable you to enter into a new level of discussion with the physician customer.

This is the most prevalent and pervasive aspect of psychiatry in general medicine. The worker's compensation patient who subconsciously exaggerates symptoms from a job injury, the person who complains of migraine headaches because she is stressed at work, and the man with chest pain admitted to the ICU to rule out a myocardial infarction whose symptoms turn out to be "stress" and not caused by a heart attack, all fall under the umbrella of somatization.

The term "somatization" was first defined early in the 20th century as a "deep-seated" neurosis causing physical problems. The modem definition is essentially the same: "the tendency to experience and communicate bodily (somatic) distress and symptoms unaccounted for by pathological findings, to attribute them to medical illness, and seek medical help as a result." This tendency is usually in response to some stressful life event. In general, the patients do not recognize the source of their problems as psychological and may resist any reassurance that they are physically healthy. They may "doctor shop," convinced they will find the clinician who alone is capable of giving them the medical diagnosis that others repeatedly miss. There are several specific types of somatization disorders:

A **hypochondriac** will tell their doctors the exact diagnosis they have, and seek medical confirmation over and over. One fellow I've seen is convinced he has HIV (he has never had sex, never used IV drugs, and is only 17). One could argue he has a type of paranoid delusional disorder or an obsessive compulsive disorder, but antipsychotics, and anti-O/C drugs have not prevented him from going to one emergency room after another and getting at least 15 HIV tests! Their repeated "negative" result does not stop him from seeking other opinions. He feels that he has repeated infections (colds, flu's), and believes that HIV is the only explanation!

The classic somatization disorder is the **conversion reaction**. Actually rare, it involves a person's subconscious creating a medical symptom to allow them to avoid some particular stress. If you have a big exam at the end of a sales training conference, and you wake to find your arm is paralyzed that morning, you have a conversion disorder. In the documentary film "A Fighter Pilot's Diary," a WWII pilot describes strafing two truck loads of Nazi soldiers, and when he flew back over to survey the carnage, his right arm "froze." (He had to land his plane with only one functional arm, but did recover hours later.) This pilot's reaction to killing a few dozen people was to subconsciously make sure it didn't happen again anytime soon. As in these two examples, the complaints usually involve motor or sensory deficits, suggesting some neurological pathology, however, symptoms don't conform to known anatomical pathways, but follow an individual's conceptualization of a condition. Interestingly, patients often display an indifferent attitude, seemingly unaffected by the seriousness of their symptoms.

A patient with a factitious disorder or **Munchausen's syndrome** is motivated to actually seek the patient role, and often will induce illness in order to become a patient. Some inject themselves with materials to deliberately cause an infection, or may even tear open surgical wounds. Though their injuries are self-inflicted and obviously consciously produced, the motivation underlying these actions is the desire to assume the role of a medical, surgical, or even psychiatric patient (one man travels our state going from one psychiatric hospital after another and says he "hears voices..." He just really enjoys being on a psychiatric ward and getting antipsychotics!). Issues of financial reward or disability status are not motivating factors. This is differentiated from consciously producing injury for financial gain or time off work, which is simply malingering (i.e. faking medical symptoms "to cheat the system").

The factitious disorder presentation is quite complicated, as patients may fabricate subjective complaints, self-inflict conditions, or exaggerate existing medical conditions, or present with any combination of these three. Chronic hospitalizations are characteristic, often patients will leave the hospital against medical advice when confronted with their diagnosis or when they suspect they'll be detected. Some present to different physicians and hospitals giving different names. The popular press has recently highlighted Munchausen's syndrome "by proxy," a condition in which a parent will act out this pathology by making the child ill, and subsequently seeking medical help. The victim is usually a preschool child, although adults have been victimized as well. Perpetrators are usually mothers who have some experience in health care, and they often seem aloof or inappropriately unconcerned about the reported illness.

These are the well defined somatization illnesses, but there are many more clinical encounters that are less defined. Take for example, non-cardiac chest pain. This is an illness in which the person seems to be having a heart attack, but they are not. All the symptoms are there, chest pain, shortness of breath, anxiety, but when admitted to the hospital, their heart is found to be normal. Their cardiac vessels may be completely patent too. But in medicine, we rule out the most dangerous things first, and then look for less lethal causes. We've studied these patients who were admitted with chest pain but fortunately did not have heart attacks. A survey as they left the hospital asked for their impression of "what really happened to you?" And ⅓ believe that they had a heart attack (when they didn't), ⅓ say they were told it was "stress," and the rest aren't sure what happened! In medicine, we are great at finding and treating heart attacks, but when the tests are negative, we obviously have a lot to learn.

Why is all of this clinical information important to you? Because the "gray zones" of medicine are where the science of the practice takes a back seat to the art of practice. In our day to day lives, we see all sorts of illnesses that are poorly defined, or involve some mixture of physical and psychological pathology. Some studies estimate that 60% of the people who see primary care physicians are there for some type of somatization.

Does this mean you as the representative should forget about your knowledge of cardiology or hypertension? Of course not, *that* is the framework from which both you and your customer work. But appreciate that your customer is seeing a complex mixture of psychology and medicine every day.

Now you know more than most doctors about the complex area of somatization!

What are some of the ways to use this knowledge?

1. It gives you a way of understanding and discussing drug non-responses. If a physician tells you they've had little luck with your product, you could explore with the doctor exactly how those patients present. For example, a lady recently reported no benefit from her anti-depressant. When the rep visited me and asked how things were going with the product, one I don't use too often, I was reminded of this patient. But I told the rep that no antidepressant would work as long as her husband refused to get treatment for his alcoholism. Of course we still treat her depression despite the continued stress, but our expectations are different.

2. This knowledge can give you a new perspective about your product that docs will appreciate. You will approach sales with the understanding that one drug does not fit all. We like that. It means you'll stand apart from the reps who think we should put everyone on the same drug.

3. An understanding of somatization opens the door to advanced educational opportunities. If you detail a neurologist on an anticonvulsant,

you are well versed on all types of epilepsy and treatments, and so is the doc. It is a bit routine for both of you. But ask them if they need a CME program on definitive treatment strategies for pseudoseizures (patients whose seizures are psychologically produced, and not epileptic). They will line up!

Reflect on:

Doctors in my territory who appreciate the psychological component to illness are ______________________.

chapter

# 18 The Silent Partner in Patient Care

I've had the privilege of seeing Mark MacGuire hit a grand slam (and against Gregg Maddux), seeing the Royal Shakespeare Company perform Macbeth, and even heard Yo Yo Ma. Some people simply take their craft to the next level. But I have also seen great pharmaceutical reps and sales trainers in action.

Even though these jobs are not publicly displayed, I've seen them performed at the highest level.

So what is the next level in pharmaceutical sales?

In a sentence: **you become a partner in patient care.**

I'll give you an example — There are a few representatives in my town that are functioning at a level so far above the competition, that they actually help many of my patients get better. Now, they will never know those patients, but they provide me with the knowledge and help I need in a timely fashion.

One of those reps, Kerry, once got on his cell phone while sitting in our waiting room to call his medical department at the home office. I had a patient in front of me and needed to know if his drug was safe with her experimental hepatitis treatment. Within a few minutes I had the answer, and she got the drug I felt was best for her. He also helped to get a patient in an indigent drug program that prevented countless seizures. This patient often cut back on her epilepsy medication to save money, and of course her blood level would frequently drop to sub-therapeutic. Those are just a couple of the many grand slams he's hit for me.

We can learn a lot from Kerry. These are the methods he uses to rise to the next level:

1. Each call is an opportunity to serve the customer and the patient at a higher level.
2. Be aware! You'll never notice an opportunity if you're not looking for one.
3. He never says "May I help you with that?" always "I WILL help you with that..."
4. Be mindful of your resources — indigent programs, drug information (printed and by phone), and so on. Have your support numbers handy — your support is my support.

And remember, there is no shame in being a silent partner. Reagan said, you can accomplish a lot if you don't care who gets the credit for it.

Once you develop this mindset and listen to that voice inside that pushes you to the next level, you'll sense something odd. No matter how hard you work there really is no "level." There is no platform of superior work you operate from. As you become that partner in care, and live and work at the higher level, the level then moves even higher. You will notice more and more opportunities to excel. The goal is elusive, and it should be. Never trust the representative who says they have "done all they can" or they are already at the highest level possible. The good strive for the best, the great never quit striving for better.

But, is there another level beyond "the silent partner in patient care ?"

Yes...

*chapter*

# 19

# *The Silent Business Partner*

When I was publishing my first book, I told one of my reps about the difficulties. I explained that finally I knew how a rep felt. I had to gain access to fellow physicians and get their opinions on detailing strategies. Even though most of them knew me as a friend, I still had to buy them dinner to get their opinions! But, to create a quality book, I needed research, and I was willing to pay for that quality.

The rep who heard all this had an idea. If some of the research on medical decision making would benefit his company, he could get me a small grant to help cut down on the costs. It was a win-win-win situation: I got the data I needed, he further built a relationship with me, and his company got research that helped shape their next marketing approach.

This is why he's a top rep: all of the reps I saw that week heard my jokes about how I was the "rep for a day," but he saw these remarks as an opportunity — he actually became a partner in my business development.

When I ask doctors to list the typical qualities they see in reps, they respond with: "intelligent, motivated, energetic, and people oriented..." Who wouldn't want a business partner like that?

What are the ways you can help develop the businesses of your customers?

Think about your key doctors as you examine this list:

**Ways to Become the Silent Business Partner:**

- Are there grants for community based research in a physician's area of interest?
- Would any of your doctors be passionate and energetic speakers on behalf of your product?
- Are there opportunities for key doctors to consult with your company?
- Can you be the liaison for networking a key doctor with referral sources in their community? (And, are those sources also supporting your product?)
- Are your key doctors always invited to update meetings about your product?

## *The Last Word:*

Obviously, there are limits to what you should and can do in helping your physician customers, but as you go about your next work day remind yourself to look for opportunities to become that silent partner.

"And our marketing team is putting the final touches on their projections for the upcoming year..."

*chapter*

# 20

# *Unknown Strategies That Increase Market Share*

One of my recent consultations involved a great product that had a very large market share, so I was a bit surprised that I was asked to help. I thought "this market share is excellent, and it will be hard to improve on... " My first impression was that most patients who could benefit from the product were already on it, as it had been out for several years and was always heavily marketed.

But after some initial research, I realized the huge market share reflected the quality of the product, and there are always more patients who can benefit from one of the best, and I set out to find new ways to get the word out and promote the drug. Here are the results:

1. **Use Your Local Media:** Local media can be your friend. Just as "all politics is local," all of your market share is local too. So, consider that when a local paper runs an article on your product, or a t.v. talking head does a story on "beating high cholesterol" or "beating winter blues," this can mean hundreds of folks go to the doctor in the

next few days and say "I heard about drug X..." One example occurred recently in our community. I was asked to contribute to the health section of the local paper one weekend, and I answered one particular question that had been submitted about a new antidepressant. Three patients actually brought the article in to their appointments and showed it to me. They asked to be put on this wonderful new drug, but most of them didn't bother to read the author's name, and had no idea I wrote the article! (Now, not every doctor can write, and many are terrible on camera, but the local medical society can usually direct you to charismatic members of the medical community. And some of your companies may even have arrangements with PR firms who find activities like this that promote your product.)

2. **Exploring Untapped Markets:** You spend your day calling on physicians because we are the ones who write most of the prescriptions. But it may surprise you to learn that in some settings, we simply supervise other prescribers. Contrary to popular belief, the biggest change as far as "who prescribes drugs" is not from physician over to psychologists or pharmacists as the press likes to debate, but to nurse practitioners and physician assistants. They function indepen-

dently in many settings, and make sole treatment decisions in some cases. Rather than invite these folks to dinner programs along with physicians, why not sponsor a dinner for them? Many nurse practitioner or physician assistant societies hold regular meetings that are eager for sponsors. Also, there are some settings where a few key clinical decision makers control the prescription patterns such as in nursing homes or extended care wards. I help out at our hospice inpatient center, and it may surprise you to learn that the nurses really make most of the treatment decisions. And why not? They spend 24 hours a day with the patients, I just pop in once or twice a week. So when they call me and say, "We'd like to try Mr. Jones on drug X," I always order it... So, try tending to the traditionally neglected decision makers in health care.

3. **Hosting "One to One" Dinners:** I was once flown to a city just to have dinner with one doctor and his wife. I even got to bring a date! Why? Because he is an important thought leader in our specialty. He couldn't come to the CME program the week before, so a private dinner was arranged. Now this may seem like overkill, but if he's on board with a product, many other doctors will follow his lead. He also is assigned to the formulary committee at his hospital.

Customers like this have a lot of influence. I'm sure you can recite the top prescribers in your territory who are not on board, why not arrange a private meeting with a doc who is a supporter of your product?

4. **Turn Your Customers Into Researchers:** In medicine, there is an old saying — there are doctors who treat patients and doctors who write about treating patients. But the new reality is that many academic doctors see plenty of patients, and many in private practice will publish. When a doc tells you about an interesting case involving your product, encourage him or her to write about their experience for a journal. You can even offer the services of the medical writing department of your company to help with the grit work of references and "cleaning up" the manuscript for publication. When we write about a drug, we have to research it thoroughly, and thus, we really become experts on the product.

5. **The Dynamic Speaker Program:** Don't just get a speaker, get an outstanding speaker. Network with your colleagues to find out who does a great job and really moves markets. One of my focus group sessions involved asking doctors what kind of speakers had the most influence on

> their prescription habits. The majority listed "the passionate speaker" as the most influential. When you've lined up a dynamic professional to speak for you, see if they will ride with you the day of the program to increase attendance or address questions from docs who won't make it that night. Ask if they'll ride with you the next day as well. See Chapter 12 for more strategies on successful speaker programs.

Back to my consultation. Did it work? So far, the market share has been rising in the territory where these strategies have been implemented.

**Summary of Main Points:**

- Use your local media to promote your product. Though this strategy is done indirectly, such as physician written health articles or news spots, your company may already have a PR firm helping with promotion. Your job is to get the doctors who are supportive of your product lined up with these firms.
- Don't neglect nurse practitioners, PA's, or residents and students.
- Never underestimate the power of 1 to 1 time between professionals. Arrange for visiting experts to talk to local thought leaders and high prescribers. Don't be afraid to ask; I've flown a long way for dinner.
- When a doctor reports a great case involving your drug, encourage them to get the word out and publish. You can establish a contact with your medical science liaisons.
- When I write an article on a drug, I then become an expert on it.
- Get passionate, dynamic speakers — then utilize their talents to the fullest.

# *About the Author:*

Dr. Andy Farah was born in Charleston, SC, attended Clemson University, and then The Medical University of South Carolina. He completed his residency in psychiatry at The Bowman Gray School of Medicine at Wake Forest University in 1994. He practices general psychiatry in the Triad of NC, lectures widely on psychopharmacology, and has contributed to numerous clinical and business publications. He first began researching medical decision making in 1992.

# *Seminar Information:*

Dr. Farah is available for consultations regarding sales and marketing strategy. He has spoken to numerous training sessions about the physician customer, and specific product selling strategy.

He also is available for the lectures: *The Accidental Leader©* and *The Pyramid of Leadership©* which are designed to help reps and pharmaceutical company employees effectively handle new leadership responsibilities, and provide the basics for future growth in management.

# *How to Reach Dr. Farah:*

phone (336) 664-9218
fax (336) 931-1367
E-mail drandyfarah@yahoo.com

address:
Farah Consulting
8755 Bame Rd.
Colfax, NC 27235

To order more books, or *The Doctor As Customer*, simply contact Dr. Farah directly.